BD8 & Beyond

by

David Moulds

Grosvenor House
Publishing Limited

All rights reserved
Copyright © David Moulds, 2012

David Moulds is hereby identified as author of this
work in accordance with Section 77 of the Copyright, Designs
and Patents Act 1988

The book cover picture is copyright to Inmagine Corp LLC

This book is published by
Grosvenor House Publishing Ltd
28-30 High Street, Guildford, Surrey, GU1 3EL.
www.grosvenorhousepublishing.co.uk

This book is sold subject to the conditions that it shall not, by way of
trade or otherwise, be lent, resold, hired out or otherwise circulated
without the author's or publisher's prior consent in any form of binding or
cover other than that in which it is published and
without a similar condition including this condition being imposed
on the subsequent purchaser.

A CIP record for this book
is available from the British Library

ISBN 978-1-78148-540-8

Step Up To The Mark....

It was a few days before Christmas and after breaking up from work, foremost on everyone's mind was going out on the beer and partying. Bradford had always had some great pubs and a good night life but in recent years a lot of the pubs had been replaced by crappy wine bars that were full of young trendy tossers and student types and most of the 'town boys' seemed to have disappeared.

We were on a mission to let our hair down and have a top day on the booze. A few back street pubs with a few old mates and we were on our way into town to meet up with all the guys from work. We entered the Queens after a good gallon and we were buzzing. It was busy with Christmas 'finishers', spirits were high and the atmosphere was tripping. There were five of us in our direct group and the other four mingled with all our workmates while I had a chat with one of the doormen, who I'd known for a number of years. After a couple of drinks, everyone started to move to the next pub, I was with my mate Si and after bidding John, the bouncer, farewell, we went to catch up with the crowd. As we approached the next bar, there was a little bit of a queue and as we got to the door, Si started to enter but one of the two Asian doormen said I'd had too much to drink and couldn't come in. I tried to explain that I hadn't and had a dodgy knee but they were so arrogant and full of themselves and were having none of it. A couple of mates came out and after a short conversation, common sense prevailed and we persuaded the two 'jobsworths' to let me in. Less than half an hour later and it was time to move on but on the way out, one of the doorman thought he'd make a few smart 'quips' and have a laugh on our behalf. Well, words were exchanged and the smaller of the two doormen took a cheap shot and punched me on the back of my head, as I turned, the cheeky 'tool' digged me straight in the middle of the cheek. Well all hell broke loose and the two fellas had to earn their pay, or, rather not! I managed to land a decent shot on my assailant and sent him flying backwards, his partner, who was a lot taller and a bit of a boxer, so I learned later, came forward and although I was stood a step lower down, I caught him with an uppercut that went straight through his guard and he ended up with an open wound from his eye to his hairline. These two had opened a hornet's nest and got well stung as three or four, pissed off guys got weighed into them. They were very good with the verbal but after having the shit knocked out of them in the foyer, they ended up running into the bar, crying for help and covered in 'claret'. Start it.......... finish it.

Unfortunately for me, it hadn't crossed my mind that the two so called 'doormen' would get the law and start searching all the pubs in the surrounding area but hey ho, that's exactly what these two clowns did and inside the hour, both Si and myself were sat in the cold cells for the rest of the night.......................

Just another unfortunate day in the life!

INTRODUCTION

I've always had the conception that if you start a brawl, fist fight or bring violence into an argument of any kind, then you should accept the consequences. The result being that you either win, get your arse kicked or end up having to deal with the law. On the other hand, if you don't start an incident and end up winning, then, in my opinion, that's perceived as self defence and the other bloke should accept what he receives but unfortunately, the law doesn't work like that and they will, more often than not, try to nick you. I believe there's a quote that states "Your human right to swing a punch, stops where another man's nose begins"............. that pretty much says it all.

In no way whatsoever is any part of this book aimed at glorifying violence at any level, or in any shape or form. It's just an insight into my life and how, for a long time, there always seemed to be someone stood in the way, wanting to have a piece of me for one reason or another.

When working on the doors, I always did my best to try and defuse any incident or any confrontation by using a non-physical approach but that approach isn't always effective and sometimes the use of physical force is the only option. In some circumstances, a good chat and an open mind can clear up quite a lot of disagreements but on the flip side of the coin, you can always come across some joker who thinks this is a sense of weakness and decides to take a pop at you. Reasonable force is then brought in but if the situation is getting out of hand and your own, along with other people's safety is likely to be jeopardised, then the force needed to quash an incident may have to be to taken up a level.

In life I believe that a person will have five or six top friends, these friends are for life and are mates that you don't necessarily have to see on a regular basis but they'll always be there, when needed……forever. I have my six top mates, some of who I see on a regular basis and some that are in contact but I don't see too often, the bond is there and these guys all know who they are without me having to go all soppy and blurting out a load of old mush. That statement doesn't mean that one can't have hundreds of friends, it's just my opinion that a handful are at a different level and in the pages ahead, there are a hell of a lot of friends mentioned.

"Friendship is sometimes like money, easier made than kept"……………albeit, that quote doesn't apply to the half dozen who are 'bonded' forever.

Chapter 1

Being brought up in the Girlington area of Bradford in the 60's wasn't a hardship at all, the area wasn't that rough at the time and most of my childhood was as pleasant as the next kids. All the families around the back street where we lived were quite close and if you were ever out of order, there was always somebody's mum ready to clock you one round the back of the napper. That was always accepted and when you're mum found out, you were usually on the end of another slap. My mum had a flat wooden bat with a little hole in the handle which was hung on a hook in the kitchen. On the bat was a picture of a 'Bambi' and the inscription that said "for the cute little deer with the bare behind", if we were out of order, we would feel the sting of that bat right across our backsides and boy did it hurt, mum was pretty handy with that implement! Mum and dad worked all hours to make sure we had as much as any other kid, Pam, my sister, was born in 1958; sixteen month before me, brother Pete was born twenty months later than me and brother Bryan was born much later in 1967. Kids at that time new the 'rights' and 'wrongs' of everyday living and almost all respected their elders, what parents said was 'right' and you didn't answer back as such. BD8 was no 'Hell's Kitchen' and if you kept your nose clean, there was nothing to worry about.

Every Saturday, until I was about eight, we took it in turns to go to my Nan's house for the day, two of us would go and the third stayed at home, Bryan wasn't in the frame then. My granddad would always take us into Peel park and occasionally, we'd run through Undercliffe cemetery, which was where they filmed the Billy Liar picture, with Tom Courtney..........happy days, young kids with no cares or fears.

In those days, most adults seemed to smoke, all advertisements seemed to be smoking related and almost everyone on TV or in a film had a cig in their mouth. Every morning and afternoon, all the mothers in our back street, would nip round to one house for a brew and once they'd all lit their smokes, you couldn't see a damn thing. How times change, these days you're thought of as some kind of leper if you smoke at all.

All the kids got on pretty well where we lived and there was a good mix of age, Kipper Dog (Brian) was the oldest kid in our street, six years older than me, and a big lad that everybody looked up to, he eventually joined the navy at 16 and that was him gone. Stephen, (Crabbo) lived over the back street from me, he was a year younger than me, we did plenty as kids but nothing really once we hit the teens. There was one incident that still has me chuckling, it was when the trolley busses were running throughout Bradford and the overhead tracks ran on Duckworth Lane, across the top of our street. It was late sixties and I'd be about 8 years old. One Saturday afternoon, there were four or five of us at the point where the directions of the tracks could be lever changed and after being dared, Stephen was lifted up by this big Polish kid called Roman and he pulled the lever. The result was that some of the track came down and the whole trolley line into town was out of order, top draw! Anyway, his name got put in the frame and I think he had a caution, probably his only ever run in with the law in his life. It's not so often to hear or see many of the kids that lived in that street these days, although one or two are still in the frame. Ian Jack (Stephen's cousin), lives high up in Scotland, working as a lock keeper or something, Martin (the Smooth) became a paramedic and I think he's in Cumbria and Billy Fish moved to Rotherham but now lives up at Denholme, Phil Hartley part owns a bakery business I think and Stephen and his brother Graeme still live somewhere in Bradford. Others that lived there were, Mick and Graham Hughes, Julie and Elaine Ansell and Steve Hebden.

For a couple of years, in the summer holidays, a large group of us would go down to St Josephs College where big Roman's dad was the caretaker and use the gym facilities and the swimming pool. There were always around eight lads and a few lasses and we would spend a couple of days a week there, it was top drawer, the pool had two high diving boards and a springboard and the place was immaculate condition. The gym had everything as far as equipment was concerned and we would participate in everything from 5-aside football to building our own assault courses and running ourselves into the ground! Unfortunately our summer holiday 'gym and pool' paradise came to an abrupt halt after a couple of years as big Roman's dad hung himself in the changing room area, shame really because his dad was a nice old guy and actually put his job on the line by letting us have the freedom of the place. Roman, later, was briefly was on the books for Bradford City, as he was a decent goalkeeper but I haven't heard of or seen him since the seventies.

There was always plenty of activity in the back street between Kensington Street and Durham Road; everybody knew everyone else's business and everyone looked out for everyone else. When November approached, all the kids were out 'chumping' for firewood and stocking up for Bonfire night, almost everyone pulled their weight, young girls as well. Mick Stead, a bit of smart arse from a few streets away, once told us that a house up the Woodlands Road was getting new drive gates and the old ones were ours if we wanted them. The gates were really big, heavy wooden things that warranted a few of us to lift them and took quite a while to get them home. Once they were home, those gates were quickly smashed to bits and stored but Stead had pulled a fast one and the gates owners were soon round kicking off! Apparently, those gates weren't down to be replaced, well, not until we'd paid a visit! The parents of all the kids involved paid for new gates and we all got a whacking and had to pay back the cash over time, lesson learned......'You rarely get owt for nowt!' and never listen to a pillock like Stead! I think the Kipper Dog ended up giving Stead a smacking for his troubles.

When bonfire night arrived it was always a big street affair with everybody chipping in, there would be plenty of toffee, gingerbread, toffee apples, parkin cake etc. The bloke from the corner shop would bring a dozen bottles of pop and a rake of spice for the kids and my old man would cook all the pie and peas, it was the business. It was always an eventful time, there was a street light in the middle of the backstreet and one year the fire was too close to it and totally destroyed it, much to every kid's amusement. The fireworks were always well supervised but it was a thing for us kids to nick a few out of the tins and congregate in a garden further down the street. One year Kipper Dog and his mate Giggsy, let a rocket off and it went straight through a bathroom window, setting the curtains alight and half the bathroom. There was hell on and the old Polish geezer who lived there was actually in the bath at the time, well, the law arrived along with a fire engine, questions were being thrown around like no tomorrow but by that time we'd legged it.

Winters were tops in the late sixties to early seventies, it was nearly always a white Christmas and the snow would be at least a foot deep and seemed to last for ages. Massive snowball fights, the building of 'walls' and igloos up the backstreet were in abundance and all the kids were involved. We would sledge the full length of the backstreet, straight across the road and into the backstreet further down, with the aid of a lookout positioned on the road. It wasn't always wise to enter the bottom backstreet, there was always friction and there was a kid called Brandon Walsh had a team always ready to have a do with us, he was always a back stabbing lying little runt who never thought twice about dropping you in it. His old man was some sort of security guard who actually thought he was the Old Bill and used to patrol the back street with his Alsatian dog, acting like he was Dixon of Dock bloody Green! I reckon that Walsh kid definitely got his over the years though. Phil's ma, Mrs H, lived in the second house up from the bottom of the 'back' and she would always lay a cover of ash across the snow so we couldn't shoot into the road but this more often than not caused us to fly off the sledges and end up with bloody noses, cut chins or other injuries. She was only thinking of our safety, bless her (and she made the best Rice Krispie and Corn Flake buns for miles!!).

A few of us were in the Boys Brigade at that time and would attend Sunday bible class each week, there was always plenty going on, what with football, camping, sports days and the weekly meeting one night a week. I think, overall, we were pretty good kids and although I didn't (and still don't) believe that every thing in the bible book was half it was passed up to be, we learned a few rights and wrongs for future life.

School life was ok; I was pretty much a part of all the school sports teams, relay team, rounders team, football team and even played a bit of chess! I had a lot of close school friends at Lilycroft, young lads from that time that come to mind are Adrian Rushworth, Paul Singh, Ray Ellington, Mick Sugden, Brian Noble, to name a few, we had a few laughs in our early years of growing. Ray was a really big kid compared to the rest of us and I think he was the first Jamaican lad I'd ever seen. I remember thinking, "look at the size of this big brown kid!". Myself and Phil Hartley were pretty 'thick' together then, we were the school ball boys, which was great because on a Friday, we spent half the day on the school roof and in the surrounding gardens, collecting lost balls and then more time, going round the classrooms on a mission to return them to the rightful owners! Imagine the uproar now with the health and safety, crikey, young lads on the school roof with the teacher watching from twenty to thirty feet below!!

There was a small shop next to Lilycroft School and after school it was always packed with kids buying sweets. Phil and I thought it quite clever one day to nick a full box of 'Milky Ways' and leg it out of the shop. It was that busy, we weren't noticed. We foolishly told Crabbo about our daring 'heist' and he consequently blabbed to his ma. Now his mum, Enid, pulled us and asked us to confirm what we'd done, with the understanding that our mothers wouldn't be informed if we owned up. On returning home from school the next day, Phil and I were belted by our mothers and dragged to the shop to sort out the offence. Being conned like that by a grown-up is not something you forgive as a nine year old kid. At 11 years old, left Lilycroft Junior School and I went to Drummond Road School near Manningham. At that time there was a wall in the playground with about a 7ft drop on the other side and all the new kids were thrown straight over it, some landing with a smashed bone or two, others a little bruised and battered. Our fruit and veg man at the time was a bloke called Pitts and I got on really well with his son John, who just happened to be 'cock of the school' and a real handy fucker. Someone put it about that John was my cousin and I got a wide berth from most of the school heavies...... nice.

We moved house at this time, from the terrace house in Kensington Street into the semi-detached with a garage in Durham Road, quite a bit of an upgrade really. A few people were moving house around that time but the 'back street' boys were all still pretty good mates, Billy had two years on me and Ian had one, the 'Smooth' was a year younger than me, so we were all in separate years at school. We'd spend a lot of time cycling up and around the Yorkshire Dales then, camping or staying in Youth Hostels. Everyone seemed to be quite hospitable then and there was nearly always a friendly atmosphere and you could go most places without getting abducted, bashed, robbed or raped. We would cycle up to 50 miles in a day, stop overnight and come back the next day, throughout the summer, we'd do this most weekends. On our way to a Youth Hostel in a village called Linton in the Dales, we stopped for a rest and a bite to eat on a long stretch of road passed Skipton and spent two hours digging all the 'cats eyes' out or the road. We had hundreds of these little glass 'eyes' and on arrival in Linton, we threw them all in to the village stream and booked in at the Youth Hostel. We thought we were the cleverest kids on earth that night as we sat by the bridge smoking No6 cigs and watching the moonlight shooting in all different directions off the 'eyes' in the water, it was like the Northern Lights, a bit of a bummer for the motorists driving on that road at the time though!!

Mum passed her driving test shortly after we moved into Durham Road and we got a navy blue Ford Corsair, which was the bee's knees at the time, it was washed and polished every week without fail. We always had a family holiday every year, usually, Blackpool or Morecombe, used to love them as a kid and it was nearly always a belting summer. Once we were at Butlins, Filey and I won the five year olds flat race and got a free holiday, tops! We also won the 'Family of the Week' award. Mum and Dad were over the moon and we went back the next year. My dad took up the driving lessons but he was bloody hopeless, sacked it after driving over a mini roundabout and never learned to drive at all! Mum would always take the family out in the motor but more often than not you had to make your own way to wherever and that meant the bus or on your own pins. I'd walk to school, which was about a couple of miles hike and never thought anything about it, although that would kill most youngsters today. My best mate at school then was a short lad called Keith Gardener; we would walk to my house at lunchtime and then back to school, for the afternoon classes. Kicking our heals on the long main road, we would puff away on our No 6 cigs, thinking we were really cool pieces of work but when you're 12 years old you never seem to see much of what's really going on around you and tend to live in your own bubble. One lunchtime, we hadn't noticed my mum, who was on her way home for lunch from work. She was on the bus and passed us while we were puffing away on our nicotine, well, no need to say that the shit hit the fan on my arrival at home!

We took up cross country running, Keith and I, Paul Grieg and a lad called Mark Minton, both at school and also at a running club called Bingley Harriers. We weren't brilliant but it kept us fit and I won the championship at Drummond school, setting a course record at the time. I also played football for the school, I was just average at that as well really but I think at that age, everyone thought they were better than they were and imagined they were the next George Best.

After a school games session, Keith, Mark and myself once came across a large skull, half buried in a hillside near the sports fields, so we dug the damn thing up and took it to the museum at Manningham Park (now Lister Pak). The press came to school and took our photograph for the local rag. The skull was from a couple of hundred year old cow that had large horns and was rare enough for them to keep it in the museum, on show, for quite a while. Fame for the day

Keith, myself and Paul went away camping with the Boys Brigade. At Springbank the venue was always

Ingleton and in the summer, there was always a week at the coast. One year Bridlington was the venue and I recall there was quite a bit of trouble, with the local lads mugging and bullying anyone from outside the area. I was with Mark Gledhill and we were grabbed by some local kids who knocked us about a bit near the sea-front. Luckily, a moment or two later, the cavalry came round the corner. Paul Grieg and all the 'black 'guys from the 'brigade' chased the local tossers off. The Jamaican sector of our Boys Brigade were the Oxford brothers, the Dacres and one or two others. These were sound lads who we wee friends with for a long time and knew though the brigade and school. On that camping trip was a guy called John Whytell, who was probably about seventeen at the time. He was a bit of a lad and was always trying to pull skirt but was also a bully and actually a total knob when it came down to it. One day whilst in the town centre of 'Brid', Keith and I saw him nipping into an ale house for a jar or two. Later on the Brigade mini bus, he was sat facing us and we said we'd seen him earlier that day but he denied being in the centre and said we were mistaken. Just as I said he was going into the boozer, the bastard kicked me under the chin, busting my lip. Very clever, to level a young kid like that and if I'd have met the twat in my 'pomp', we'd have definitely had words! Other, older lads in the Brigade at the time said that he was regarded as a bit of a bully boy. The 19th Bradford Brigade was run by Fred Williams and he was a truly great man, fair but firm and as the Brigade motto stated 'Steadfast & Sure'.

Nearly every Saturday, from being eight years old, we went to Valley Parade, home of Bradford City, we would watch the first team, and then the following week, we would watch the reserves. My cousin Richard played for the reserves, so for those games, my dad, brother Pete and I would sit in the decent seats. For my twelfth birthday, my dad asked what I wanted and I said that I would like to go and watch Leeds in the first division, as Bradford played in the third. I think every kid picks his team about that age and after seeing Leeds win 2-1 against Tottenham Hotspur at Elland Road, I was and still am, Leeds through and through. My brother Pete chose the red of Manchester, absolute nightmare, as my dad also had a thing for them. My mum never bothered with the footie, although she did date one of the Busby Babe, Duncan Edwards in the mid fifties, a couple of years before the Munich air disaster. Some top barnies about Leeds/Man United would follow down the years in the Moulds' household, make no mistake.

In 1973 I went to Rhodesway Grammar School and the initiation there was literally to be thrown down a steep hill next to the playing fields. No way round that, within three days of being there, I was launched down the hill but luckily, ended up with only a few bruises. A lad called David Moore, who was in our form, ended up with stitches in the bottom of his back and a few more lads ended up with more than bruises. I'd was also on the end of the headmasters cane in the first week, for fooling about outside his office, Mr Styles was his name and the old fucker didn't have a sense of humour at all, as I was to find out over the next three years, after feeling the swish of his cane on several occasions.

I was just above the average 'John Smith' at school really, reasonably bright, played for the football team and did the cross country/athletics. I became the first kid from Rhodesway to run for the Bradford schools cross country team, which got big accolades because the school was mainly well known for producing boxers for the English Schools Team. I also ran for Bingley Harriers, running up to around seventy miles a week and racing most weekends up and down the country. I even managed to win the Boys Brigade cross country championship in Bradford twice and came fifth in the National Boys Brigade Championships. That all basically was shelved when I started working, drinking and more smoking.

I suppose I played truant as much as the next 'normal' kid really but most of the time, I knuckled down and tried to do the studying thing. There was one afternoon in October 1975 when Dave Moore, Paul Greig, Steve Coyle, My brother Pete and his mate, all bunked off to go to Elland Road to get tickets for the Leeds v Man U league game. We went through on the train from Bradford and queued at the ground to buy the tickets, then we all forged sick notes to take to school the next day. Myself and Dave were Leeds and the other four were Scumchester 'Reds', we lost 2-1, what a shitter. Coming back to Bradford on the train, I got my first, up-close, look at some of the 'Red Army'. The train dropped at Bradford and then went onto Manchester and was full of proper 'boys' that I would be having one or two toe to toe's with later in life. When we got home, I bashed brother Pete for all the smart shite he came out with after the game.

That year, just after Christmas, I went with Billy Fish and Ian, from the backstreet, up to Ingleton in the Yorkshire Dales to camp over the New Year. The views up there are breathtaking, no matter what time of year it is and you can easily drift into another world and dream away. The first day was ok but after that, the wind and snow set in and we were in serious shit. We had two tents that were joined together with quite a large fly sheet as a sort of entrance area and thought all our kit was adequate for the winter weather. The first night was fine but the next day, the winds were up and the blizzards set in. We set off with packs on and made our way down into Ingleton.....felt like Captain Scott and his crew heading for the North Pole!!! When we arrived in the town, we were wet through and well weather beaten, this was certainly not the kind of winter break that we had in mind. We dried off some of our kit in the local washerette, had a bite to eat in one of the cafés and started to head back up into the hillside. We decided to use the road route, rather than cutting corners by crossing fields or going up the 'falls' route but it was still dusk when we arrived back at our campsite. That night was an absolute nightmare, the wind and snow blizzards were knocking the hell out of our tents and we knew it was only a matter of time before the weather got the better of us. Billy and I were in one tent and Ian was in the other, we were plying ourselves with cans of lager and miniature bottles of spirits, while at the same time hanging onto the tent poles for dear life! We thought it best that we should all three secure one tent but Ian (the selfish bastard) said it was every man for himself!! Both me and Billy piled into his tent and after Ian copped for a bit of a slap, all three of us were holding one tent down. We managed to get a couple of hours sleep but on opening the tent door in the morning, the results of the snowstorm's wrath were clearly apparent. The snow was about three foot deep and the adjoining fly sheet, along with the second tent were strewed against a farm wall approximately one hundred yards away!! Well, hence to say, we were soon home and spending the New Year back in Bradford.

Chapter 2

Visiting the Careers Officer at school was a joke really in those days. The options were, the Army, a factory job or a supermarket!! If you mentioned anything other than those options, the officer just frowned at you and told you there was no way that a kid from your background and schooling would ever be paid to do anything else. Quite scandalous really but those arseholes were paid to advise you only what the system had planned out for you. I left school at 16 and after applying for various career options, got a start at Renolds, Croft Gear Works in Bradford. I'd seen the odd position advertised in the press and I enquired but to no avail. A cartographer job in Bristol and a Diving Maintenance job in Southampton were two careers I tried for but got knocked back from both. I'd been on a school trip to Portsmouth to visit the Naval base and quite fancied a career in the Navy. After visiting the careers office in Leeds I was sent over to Manchester for interviews and tests. A full day there, only to be told that because of red/green colour blindness, there was no career whatsoever in the Navy. A load of old knacker I thought, I'm sure there was an opening but the over weight bloke I dealt with wasn't about to put himself out for me.... Bollocks to your damn Navy!

I'd passed 'O' levels in maths and technical drawing and was hoping to start as a draftsman but the short little fat guy doing the interviewing at Renolds said that because I didn't have a physics qualification, the only position available to me was on the craft side, working on the shop floor. So that was me, apprentice engineer with overalls, steel toecap boots and that well known stink of oil and grease about me! Bit of a shitter really because today, there's probably only a handful of draftsmen in the country that can use a pencil, board and 'T' square, everything is done on Cad or similar type systems on the computer these days.

There were over 30 apprentices taken on each year at that time at Renolds and there were two sections of training schools to endure before you reached the shop floor. There were plenty of accidents and a third never crossed the finish line but there were some good times and we were taught our trades well. The bar staff at the work's social club would overlook the fact that we were under age and we could get a gallon of bear for a couple of quid....good days! We had to wear caps with hair nets on the back when working near machinery, which was a real bind, so one Thursday teatime, after being paid, a trip to the local barbers was in order. My brother Pete, who had well long hair then, thought he'd make one in and get shorn as well. Walking out into the fresh air, we were in hysterics rolling around howling at each others little 'peanut' heads! Ma went mental, shouting and bawling, saying we looked like a pair of evil convicts; we got the scowl and silent treatment for a few days after that.

There was a boozer round the corner from where we lived called The Royal, the landlady was Jean and her husband was John Celebanski, the boxer who sparred with Richard Dunn when he was preparing to meet Ali for the world title. I got on well with Jean and John but if ever I was out of line, I found myself face down on the cobbles outside after big John had launched me, which actually happened more than once. Fuck me; he was a big fit bloke in those days!! It was one of a few decent little back street pubs in Girlington at the time, others that we frequented around there were, the Round Thorn, the Girlington, the George and the Travellers Rest. All could be rough manors if you weren't a little bit streetwise. The Travellers Rest was run by an ex-copper who always came across as a bit of a smart arse really and seemed to think he was the king of fucking England, it was like he was doing you a great favour by letting you drink in his pub. It was also used by the plod from the Duckworth Lane Police station, just on the road, a couple of the plod being the landlords sons! Hence, we were thrown out more than once and ended up being barred over fuck all if I recall correctly, something to do with having no respect for the landlord. I think I remember telling the old twat that respect had to be earned, or something to that tune!

Music was changing rapid at that time and there were Punks with big spiky hair do's and all the colours of the rainbow but there were very few guys with a skinhead around. I'd gone into town at the weekend with Billy and a couple of other mates for a few bears, there weren't many ale houses we could get served in and we were minding our own business in the Painted Wagon stood at the bar with a pint. I heard this guy shouting about skinheads and when I looked round, I realised he was meaning me and was heading towards the bar. He was an average build kid with dark hair and was blurting 'fucking skinheads! Do you think you're handy then?'

I thought, ' there's no doubt, he's gonna clip me here', so I stepped forward and put one straight on his button. Down he went like sack of shit and a couple of his mates picked him up and pulled him away...apologising to me!! Nobody else said anything and we left shortly after, me, smiling to myself and thinking 'I am not taking shite from muppets like him', a turning point in my life.

In the seventies, most factory environments were totally run by the unions and everyone had their individual jobs to do, it was always 'that's not my job' or 'you can't touch that, that's his job'. What a right load of bollocks.........no wonder the majority of industry went to the wall in this bloody country. We went to college one day a week and learnt our trades on the shop floor during the rest of the week. It was without doubt that apprentices were used by management as cheap labour because, most of the time, we were contributing as much as the so called skilled men alongside us.

I was still doing the footie on Saturdays, all home games at Elland Road and on the road to away matches the following week. Leeds were starting to go off the boil at that time but had a big home crowd and a quality away crew that were a match for any other mob in the country. We'd gone away to Portman Road at Ipswich and seven of us thought it would be a laugh to infiltrate their end......no boys at Ipswich...surely! How fucking naïve were we! I was with Mal form work (who later joined the fire service), little Crooky, Neil Roscoe, Graham and two other lads that were always on our away coach. Just as the players came onto the pitch, we started chanting Leeds verbal; a circle appeared around us and a bit of a stand off resulted with us screaming at all the 'tractor' drivers to have a go! Fists and boots flying everywhere, with us holding our own and then the tide well turned as couple of hundred meatheads from the back of their kop charged down to piss right on our party. We took a bit of a spanking before making it to the wall behind the goal, and then managed to scramble onto the pitch. The massive Leeds contingent at the other end sang their appraisal and we were escorted down the touchline, slightly worse for wear but heroes for the day. The football violence was in full flow at that time and there were many casualties at a lot of games. We played Wolves away in the quarter final of the F.A. cup that year and that was another day that had major incidents throughout. On arrival in Wolverhampton, most of our coaches were bricked by their boys and there were violent confrontations from where the coaches were parked and up to the ground. The Leeds hoards were in one half of the big North Bank end in the Molineux ground and were segregated by a blue line of coppers, which was nowhere near enough considering the size of the crowd in that end. From the off, there battling from top to bottom on the terrace and missiles were being sent into both sections. One lad next but one to myself and 'fireman' Mal, got hit with a dart in the shoulder and another lad got a dart in the cheek, after that we quickly moved down the terrace but missiles such as stones darts and those 'Chinese' stars were consistent throughout the game. Eddie Gray headed the only goal of the game and Leeds was in the hat for the semi finals. Coming out of the ground was much the same and I got caught up in 'no mans' land, between the Leeds and Wolves fans right outside the exits. I was caught in two minds whether to stand or get back into the Leeds ranks but my mind was soon made up when a police horse galloped through and knocked me straight on my shitter, hell, it was like being run over by a fucking car!!.......out of there, rapid. We drew Scumchester United in the semi finals at Hillsborough, Sheffield and everybody was geared up for a serious 'set to' with the Mancs! The Leeds Service Crew had become a decent firm and there were punch ups all over Sheffield before and after the game with the Man U boys, even though Leeds was seriously outnumbered on the day. There were a lot of forged tickets for the game and a couple of thousand Reds were locked outside the ground as a result. Inside the ground, we went 2.0 down early on as Hill and Coppell ran a mock, absolute nightmare, we managed to get one back in the second half but were below par and went out of the cup. There was plenty of scraps on the terraces throughout the game, two thirds of the ground was 'Red' and Leeds were struggling but it was nothing to compare with the bust ups outside the ground where the ticket less scummers were waiting. We came out straight into showers of bricks, bottles and anything else they could lay their hands on, but the sheer numbers of Leeds fans coming out of the big open end, over ran those Reds and sent the fuckers scattering in all directions. In the middle of the mayhem, a police horse sent quite a few fans sprawling and made a bee line straight for me! I had to clamber up onto the grass verge as the copper slammed the horse's back end into the wall beneath me, before hurling a rake of abuse at me and threatening to 'have' me. I would have seriously crushed if the horse had flattened me against the wall. It was pandemonium, there were bodies all over the place and boots and fists flying everywhere you looked, the law just couldn't cope and never really got it under control.

Chapter 3

The works social club at Crofts had a karate club, which held training spots a couple of nights a week, so I thought I'd give that a shot, just for the hell of it. I trained hard and was quite good at the game but I never got round to taking any belts, as all the gradings were held on a weekend and I was mostly at the Leeds games. I would do the contact bouts in training and was always paired with someone of a higher grade because they knew that if I'd taken the belts, I would have been graded higher. Ian tried it but didn't last long at all, not his game but Kev Boyle, who worked with us, gave it a good go and was half decent, think he passed a few belts........haven't seen him for 20 years now. It was good for fitness and obviously, the combat aspect of it but the bubble burst on that one Sunday night in March, outside the Social club.

Billy and Ian had taken a spanking from a group of lads that used to frequent the club, on the Saturday night and were a bit worse for wear. The group were Bradford fans and we were always slagging each other off but until then, no one had come to blows. On the Saturday night in question I was out with my then girlfriend, Katrina, first love really, lovely girl but it all went pear shaped when she went to be a nanny in Jersey....oh well. Four of us, myself, 'fireman Mal, the Smooth (Martin from the back street) and Billy went in to the club on the Sunday night and three of the prats from the previous evening were sat there, smug as fuck, with big grins on their faces. Words were spoken on both sides but as there was a band on stage, a physical confrontation was put on hold. One of the committee blokes said, that under no circumstances was there to be any 'fisty cuffs' on the premises. Their main kid was a lad called Rhodes, he worked at Crofts and wasn't a half bad lad really but this had to be sorted and we went outside into the car park with the other lads close behind. It was snowing like hell and Rhodes butted me straight in the middle of the 'clock', breaking my nose and sending me reeling backwards.......can't fault him there, he was quick off the mark! Anyhow, a few minutes later, he'd got his and ended up lying 'star fished' in the snow, covered in claret, as a bit of a scuffle went on with his two mates. Three or four committee men came running out with a couple of big karate black belt guys, all shouting and bawling at us, hence to say, we made our exit and did one.

Now. In life, people sometimes tell you something and actually mean something totally different, such as the committee bloke that said we had to take any confrontation off the premises to avoid getting barred. On the Monday morning at work, all the notice boards were covered with memo's stating that due to me bashing Rhodes outside the social club, everybody under the age of 21 years old, were barred until further notice, cheers Mr lying bastard committee man!! My name was mud and all the older apprentices were saying I was going to get my arse kicked, yeh right, fuck 'em!...... named and shamed then and barred from every karate club in Yorkshire apparently. Shame really because I enjoyed doing the karate, even though there were a couple of the black belt boys were bullies and always tried to hurt you. One in particular was a guy called Steel, who I think was a sixth 'Dan' and he was always full of himself (suppose you would be, if you could knock walls down!) anyway, he was one of the blokes out in the snow on that Sunday night that was shouting and bawling at us as we left the scene.

Whenever the opportunity arose, I played darts. I was a decent 'chucker' and even reached the quarter finals of the Daily Mirror under eighteens tournament in Leeds. An apprentice that I worked with called Geoff Pickles, also liked to throw a dart or two and we quite often won plenty of 'free' pints in the pubs and clubs around Bradford. On one or two occasions though, members of Working Men's clubs such as the City Band and The East Ward, took offence to us 'sharking' them and we had to fight our way out the venues! On a cold lunchtime in the late seventies, Pickles and I nipped out of work and went for a beer or two and a game of darts in a boozer called The White Bear at Thornbury in Bradford. We entered the ale house to find a good half dozen or more Teddy Boys using the darts room, whereupon, a few sharp 'quips' were made with reference to my skinhead hairstyle. We got a drink apiece and asked if we could join in their game. To cut a long story short, I hit a 180, which to say 'didn't go down too well', would be an understatement. One of the 'Elvis' lookalikes grabbed me by the collar from behind and slapped a cut throat razor against my neck, threatening to open me up for mugging them off. The trickle of blood down my throat and being well outnumbered, was enough to persuade me to back off and leave these fifties throwbacks to their own devices. As I slowly backed out of the pub, I did contemplate leaving my darts embedded in a couple of those clowns but thought better of it.........they were quite expensive Tungsten arrows!

I played football on a Sunday morning for a team called Metro Park; we were based at a boozer called the Park, in Wibsey, Bradford. One lad I worked with, Dave Winkley, a half decent midfielder, who tried to base his game on Ray Wilkins, the then Chelsea player, played in the same team. The set up was quite good but we didn't have a brilliant team and were never in the frame to win anything really. I played centre forward and wasn't half bad when it came down to it, if we got shagged 4-1, it would be, more often than not, me that scored for us. Ronnie Goldwater was the kid with the golden feet in that team but he was always looking for something better and to be fair to him, he was a cut above where we were concerned. Both myself and Wink moved to Sedbergh Boys, where we were in a half decent team and the moral there was top draw, although we were just lacking that certain something. There was a five a side competition that we won but apart from that, not much else. In two seasons there, I scored 74 goals, we still didn't win the league but were up there challenging. Sunday morning football isn't really a game for the faint hearted and you can get kicked to fuck, with serious injuries, not that all the lads who play are total dirty gets but a lot are just that competitive and what they lack in skill, they make up for with grit and passion. I still have a few small holes in my knees and shins from tackles where studs have followed through but unless you're laid out, you just get up and carry on. Not like the arse holes that we pay 30 quid or so watch on a Saturday, who fall down if the wind blows a bit strong. Pete Simmo was a great workmate pal of mine and he and Greigy, both signed up and came to play for Sedbergh, Pete played centre half and Pauly played just in front of him. There were two clubs at Sedge, ours and Sedbergh Rovers, we played them four times while I was there and always came out on top, these games were very physical and usually had a few supporters on the sidelines getting involved, Cloughy was one of their main players but wasn't too keen on the physical side, not like National Front Tony, who played for them, he was always up for it, ha, good banter and good days. We had to play a team two divisions above us, in the cup and the match was played on Tuesday evening in a snow blizzard up at Odsal in Bradford. The weather was in our favour really, they struggled to settle on the cold evening and the snow kept coming down and making it difficult to take control of the game. We were one down with about 8 minutes to go and a good clearance from our defence was headed on by Greigy, more or less on the half way line. I was onto it, struggling to keep my feet in between two defenders and running for my life towards their penalty box, the keeper came running out to shut down the angle but I managed to get a shot in and steer the ball just inside his right hand post……. Top bollocks! We were running round like we'd won the World Cup but within two minutes of the restart, there was a major cock up in our box and they were back in front. There was a right ding dong, with all our lot arguing and blaming everyone but themselves and I told the defence exactly what I thought of their fuck up. The manager and myself were then having a right set to and almost a square up over it, even while we played out the last few minutes. I didn't play many more games for Sedge after that.

Chapter 4

Another apprentice who I worked with at that time was a kid called Lee Greenwood; he lived not too far from me and had gone to Rhodesway School, same year as we did. The first night we visited the works social club, Malcolm, the steward, asked if we were new apprentices and when we replied "yes", he said "That will make you sixteen then!" (albeit, he still pulled our beers.) Anyway there a few lads slightly older than us at Crofts, who were in the Territorial Army and they reckoned it was top draw and the upshot of it was that you got paid! Lee and myself went down to Belle View Barracks in Bradford and signed up with the Duke of Wellington's T.A.V.R. infantry regiment. The Company was paired with the Keighley Company but all our weekly internal training was done at the Bradford barracks.

It was a pretty good set up at Bradford and Lee and I were soon as 'thick as thieves' with the Ravenscliffe Estate guys, they were a group of about seven lads that all came from the Yeadon side of Bradford and were all bloody barmy! Gary Siege and his cousin, big Raymond Allard, Thornton lads and 'chinky' kid, who was wick as shit with that Kung Fu stuff, made up our 'Dirty Dozen'.

We had to partake in eight 'Bounty' weekends a year, which meant you were away from Friday teatime and returned home on Sunday night, this was part of a bonus payment that you received at the end of the year. There was also a two week camp course that you had to do each year and various Saturdays, Sundays, or both throughout the rest of the year.

Well, I tried to keep the Saturday exercises to a minimum so I could still attend as many Leeds games as possible but still managed to meet my quota with regard to everything else. Shooting exercises were always eventful times and one day up on the range at Keighley moor springs to mind. There were quite a few of us from Bradford and the odd couple from the Keighley side of the company and we arrived up on the range, set for good day of shooting. It was always a good range and the furthest point was a line on the 1000 metre range. Half way through the day, whilst we were laid on the 500 metre line, one of the Ravenscliffe guys thought it would be blast if we could hit one of the sheep on the horizon! Well there were five of us in the frame and one of the poor little lamb chops got seriously blown away, needless to say, the farmer was well pissed and had to shelled out by the Ministry and the shit really hit the fan as they tried to pin the blame.......thick as thieves!

I did a two week 'carder' at the Strensel base in York, which is a 'regular' army base and they don't take too kindly to T.A boys. I was the only private from Bradford there, apart from big Raymond, who was based in the kitchens and there was one particular sergeant who took an instant dislike to me. The little twat made me go into the 'regular' side of the base to get a hair cut, even though my length was almost crew cut, on the evening I was on guard duty. I was pushed for time and legged it through to full army boys 'fortress', only to find a queue of around 20 squadies all sat polishing their boots...lovely! I raced straight to the front of the queue, explaining my situation and planted my arse in the chair, receiving a rake of abuse from the 'square bashers'. My only back up was my guard duty pick axe handle which I had a firm grip on and thought this might save my life! The barber had me totally scalped in a matter of seconds and I was out of there faster than any of those boot cleaners could put another spit on their polish!!

Out of the 360 T.A lads on that two week 'carder', there were only two to be arrested in York centre and yes, you've got it.......yours truly and Raymond! Myself and big Ray hit the town most nights and we had to be back on base by midnight at the latest, to avoid being charged. Well we got round that by bringing the guard duty lad's alcohol, in order for them to turn a blind eye; we were never too late because reveille was 6am sharp. It was the Wednesday of the second week and we were having some grief from some local guys in York centre.......they can spot army blokes at a hundred paces! Anyway, we held our own and leathered a couple of them but the local law turned up and collared us, charging us with smashing the front door of a night club, that was us, banged up for the night. We were charged under civilian law and thrown out at 5.30am, the clever gets knowing that I was on parade at 6. Made it in the nick of time but the smart arse little sergeant had already been filled in and had me running up and down like a demented chicken in front of the rest of the parade ground, saying that I'd disgraced the whole British army! Later, got find a week's civilian wages by some very sympathetic magistrates in York's courthouse, ... yeh, right!!!.

We had few visits to York whilst on exercises and had had confrontations with the local Teddy Boys, who didn't really care too much for army lads. These fuckers were, more often than not, tooled up with, either, coshes or shivs and would try and ambush us as soon as we arrived in the town centre. One of our lads received a few stitches on one occasion but overall, we dealt those 'grease balls' some serious damage and always came out on top.

The Yorkshire Dales covers 685 square miles and has some of the best countryside scenery in the British Isles, especially around Ingleton and the Settle area. One Saturday/Sunday exercise was orienteering on the tops above Settle and there was a good mix of us from both Bradford and Keighley. After spending all day legging it around the crags and fells on the moor tops, everyone got washed and changed and ventured into Settle to fill up on some well earned booze. There were quite a few of us out but myself and Olli, one of the Ravenscliffe guys, were the only two from the 'Dirty Dozen'.Anyhow, we were getting on well with the local 'totti' in one of the pubs and they invited us along to a local 'shin dig' at the village hall, much to disapproval of all the local lads. Ollie and me had these two local girls in tow and were getting threatened by the Settle 'Mafia', telling us we wouldn't get home alive!! Ha. A couple of the Keighly boys made their excuses, one saying that he was up for a stripe and didn't want any trouble and then left. Well, around midnight, after plenty of verbal, Oliver, the two girls and myself, headed outside followed by half a dozen of the local sheep chasers. It looked like we were going to have a decent set to but after standing our ground in the car park, all we got was a load more verbal, bit disappointing really. When we eventually got back to the hanger where we were bedded down it was pitch black and the 'I want a stripe' piped up with a load of crap about us managing to escape unscathed from the locals. I'd had enough of this shithead, so calculating where his squeaking chelping was coming from, I launched my 'Dealer' boot and then followed it up. The boot hit him right in the forehead and before he could move, I was firing a few big right handers into his unprotected boat race. A couple of seconds later, the lights were on and I was being restled to the floor by a couple of sergeants and a corporal.........in the shit yet again, but was well happy that bottleless twat got his.

I was always a pretty good shot, with the SLR, LMG and pistol and was asked on more than one occasion to join the shooting team, the only problem being that the competitions were quite frequent and always on a Saturday, well couldn't by-pass the footie altogether, so it was a no no. We'd gone up to Warcop in the Lake District, another regular base, for a full Saturday of shooting, range work, field targets and Northern Ireland shooting training. In the field target exercise, I had the second highest score of the day, 33 from a possible 35 points, quality, thought I was the bee's knees and again declined the shooting team. That evening we were out on the lash and as always, when there's a town full of squadies, Regs and T.A's, there were a few rucks kicking off. The full Dirty Dozen were there and we'd been having some verbal heckling throughout the day from a rake of T.A lads from Barnsley, which carried on into the evening. They'd left the boozers and gone back to the barracks before us but Ashers, Olli and one or two others decided we should smarten them up before the weekend was over. We got back to the barracks, late on and all full of lush, only to hear the Barnsley boys giving us some verbal out of the window of their bunkhouse. Well, that was enough……..we stormed straight into them, dragging most of their guys out of bed to face the music. There were fists and boots flying everywhere, with most of them laid out covered in claret and not really that much coming back at us……..joy. The bunkhouse was smashed to bits, with bodies, bedding and bunks, strewn all over the place. Within minutes there were a gang of M.P's arresting us and dragging us off to the guard house, no sleep and plenty of ear grilling for the lot of us. Next day we were in serious shit, all on charges and on 'janker' duties until the 4 tonners arrived to ship us back to Bradford.

It all came to head really when we went to a formal evening down at the barracks to receive our Bounty Weekend bonuses, only to find that most of the dirty dozen had been paid short due to all the charges we'd been on and for the damages we'd caused. I hit the roof and told them they could stuff they poxy fucking army. I was notified through the post that someone would come to collect my kit from my home address. It was a Tuesday teatime and two army Land Rovers pulled up at the bottom of my mum's drive, the fat M.P's got out, staffs in hand and stood at the gate, I threw the large kit bag, boots etc, down the drive and told them I wanted a receipt that itemised every piece of equipment. To my surprise, they did exactly that, packed it all back up and left, stating that they hadn't come for any trouble, just the kit……..sound.

Lee went off and joined the Regular Army; he lost it a bit I think after his mate was killed, whilst stood next to him on the streets of Belfast. He made sergeant and did another three or four tours of Ireland and the last I heard had married for a second time and was living somewhere down south. Three of the other lads had joined up as mercenaries and gone over seas to fight for big bucks, whilst Ashley had set up a skip-hire firm on the other side of Bradford. As for the rest, well, your guess is as good as mine, all good fun and sound days while they lasted.

Chapter 5

As apprentices at work, we were moved around from different departments in order to gain as much experience as possible, which, in later life, you realise, was much more beneficial than first thought. Bri Hudson was a year older than myself, we'd gone to the same school but never been mates until we'd met at work and started frequenting Bradford city centre together on weekends. I was still going to plenty of football, up and down the country with fireman Mal, mainly through the Wallace Arnold coach excursions from Bradford but we occasionally went with the Leeds Service Crew on the trains. The Service Crew were a top firm then and a match for any boys in the country, we were at it everywhere we went and didn't give a toss. Bri dyed his hair red and thought he was the cool as fuck, ha, he never did the footie with us, as he was a Bradford fan but spent a lot of time with their firm, the Ointment, with guys such as, Mick Jack, Jimmy Canelli, Ricky Dadd, Gilderdale, black Eric, to name a few.

Before any of our boys had purchased any motors, we would generally reach places by bus or train. In the summer of 1977, a few of us went up to Keswick in the Lake District for a camping hol and on arrival, we realised that it was 'Geordie' holiday week, tremendous! We were sat in an open air café minding our own business but the down side was that a couple of us were wearing Leeds colours. Anyway, we got well battered, I had a broken nose, two black eyes and a couple of cuts and bruises and that were in the first hour of us getting off the bus! The up side of that hol was a girl from Newcastle that we met, we were camped the other side of the Lake near a small mountain called Capbells and we had a massive camp fire going after returning from the boozer. One or two other lads and lasses who were camping nearby joined the 'party' and a couple of 'Geordie' lads brought their girls with them. Well, the 'Geordie' lads were all for sharing and we all took turns with one of their girls, she was top draw and well up for it, one after another we took her, all night and she was totally rampant.......quality. On arrival back home, a visit to the hospital was in order and they had to break my fucking nose again so that it could be set straight, face like a bloody Panda for another fortnight!

We needed wheels to get out and about really, rather than doing the town all the time and we were lucky, with both Billy and Kev (who did the karate) getting a white Ford Escort each. We went camping quite a bit, up into the Dales, Lake District, Peak District, all over the place, great times. One Bank holiday we went up to Kettlewell for a few days break got smashed at lunch and played footie in the afternoon, you know the script, and the ale houses were on set opening times then. Well, I got on one of those political soap boxes and started preaching about firing money back into British industry and giving all the jobs to young 'uns coming out of school, as jobs weren't in abundance then, with Maggie kicking the arse out of half the country. The only party at the time that had those kind of policies were the National Front, so that didn't go down too well and we ended up getting booted off the camp site by the local plod! We went over to Kilnsey Crag, my name was mud again and after filling up with ale, we slept in the two cars in a small quarry!

Leeds played Forest four times in that season, twice in the league and in the League Cup semi finals, home and away. We went down to Nottingham for the second leg of the semi finals on a Wednesday night and the fog was in abundance, traffic was really slow. The driver kept stopping on the outskirts of City to try and find out if the game was still on and eventually found out that the game was off and we should have been turned back by the law before reaching Nottingham. We were at the traffic lights near the skating rink in the city centre when around two dozen guys emerged through the fog, all carrying building bricks and proceeded to launch them at our coach! Half the windows went through and there were a few casualties, with lads getting showered in glass and hit with the bricks. We were trying to get off the coach to have a set too but the driver put his foot down and drove the bus to the main nick! The local plod gave us a hard time and you'd have thought that we'd caused the incident. We had to drive twenty odd mile up the motorway before changing coaches and by that time we were all froze half to death!

Forest was always a bit of a volatile manor and when we played them later in the season, it was no different. The game ended 1-1 and as we came out of the ground all hell broke loose in the large car park. Quite a few coaches had windows put through and there were missiles being thrown from everywhere. We were at it good style in the middle of the car park and at one point it was hard to tell who was who. I, along with quite a few others ended up in the river Trent, with the bastards bricking us in the water before the lawmen got to grips with the situation.

In the summer of '78 a few of us booked a 'Sherpa' van and made our way down to Newquay for a week of camping, Bri, Billy, Ian, Mal, Fryer, Greigy, Kev Varley and myself were all on board, great bunch of guys. The driving was split between Varley, Greigy and Fryer; I didn't drive a car until much much later. It was a fair old trek down to the bottom end of the country and took a full day but we were all in good spirits and looking forward to pulling as much skirt as possible. We got parked up just outside Newquay at a camp site and set about pitching the tents, a few tins down us and everyone clowning about and having a laugh. Mal had a brand new tent and was paired up with Fryer, he kept bollocking him and to be honest, they sounded like a pair of old 'dears', I think it took them three or four times to get the damn tent up properly. Billy was stood there looking quite confused and after a while he blurted out that he was a couple of tent poles missing, we just pissed ourselves but Billy was really put out and was far from amused. I think he'd been a bit of a pain in the arse and the result of that was that no-one would share a tent with him and his only reserve was that van! That bloody van stunk to high heaven every morning, with porn mags, beer tins and Billy's sleeping bag all contributing. We travelled all over the place in that van, even a trip down to Lands End, which basically consists of a hell of a lot of sea, rocks, cliffs, a lighthouse and a bloody café, absolutely super, we just looked at each other and were soon out of there. The word on the street had been that a place called Tall Trees was the top gaff, a brill night with loads of skirt, the only problem being that every person we asked had no idea where it was! One lunchtime, we were having a bit of a session on the ale in the centre of Newquay and a few of the lads reckoned that they were a dab hand with that fishing game. Mal, Fryer, Brian and Varley went down and booked the afternoon on a boat and off they went to test their wits against the creatures of the deep. What a laugh, the rest of us sat outside the boozer over looking the bay, taking in the view and catching some sun. when the guys came back, Kev was over the moon that he'd actually caught a fish or two but all the other three pillocks had done was barf their rings up from start to finish, bit of a waste of time for them really but the colour of their faces had us in stitches! We tried loads of boozers, clubs and afternoons on the beaches, chasing women and trying to pull but it was all in vane, we were getting absolutely nowhere. We eventually found the Tall Trees place, a couple of days before we were due to head off back home and thought that our luck had changed. All spruced up and in a couple of taxis, we headed off to what we thought would be the highlight of our week. The place was done out quite smart, a few dance floors that were each accommodating different styles of music, two or three bars and more to the point, there seemed to be quite a few spare females. We were all over this manner, chatting up birds at every opportunity, dancing, boozing and generally having a pretty decent night. Try as we may, not one of us could manage to pull any skirt, it was as if they were all having one of those 'we hate northerners' weeks! ....unbelievable. We stopped in Nottingham for a night on the piss on our way home and probably had our best night of the week, then home. At the time, we all thought it was a pretty shite week but years after, we looked back and thought differently, it was actually a half decent time.

There was a boozer/club over at Armley in Leeds called Upstairs Downstairs and we started going over there on a Tuesday night, it was a lively manor with offers on the booze and plenty of skirt around. Greigy, Billy, Kev, Fireman Mal, Dave Fryer, Ian, myself and sometimes Bri went there on numerous occasions and always had a top evening out. Billy was always a bit smart with gob and quite a few times he would end up starting some kind of kick off. I can't really remember what happened on the night in question but a few local guys were mouthing off and soon the shit had hit the fan, we were scrapping in lumps, all the way down the stairs from the top bar and into the car park. Well, we came out of it ok but hence to say, we were barred and that was the end of those Tuesday night excursions.

Saturday nights would sometimes end up at the Mecca in Bradford, a huge club that held up to 2000 punters and was always busy. Most of us were pretty naff dancers but Bri thought he was the dog's knackers and was always shooting from one side of the dance floor to the other to Northern Soul or Motown stuff. On one particular night, he got that giddy, whizzing across the stage area, he wasn't watching in the direction he was going and flew straight off the fucking stage and crashed onto a table full of drinks! Well we were literally crying with laughter as he picked himself up and tried to make out that he was ok and hadn't injured himself but truthfully, he'd nearly killed himself! We'd left the club and were heading into the centre of town to get a taxi's when we noticed quite a large group of Asian geezers, some distance behind us. They seemed to be following us so we kept a close eye on them but on reaching the taxi rank, they'd doubled in numbers and made a move on us. Massively out numbered, we had to do one but I took a wrong route and had to run through about a dozen of them. They all had their belts in their hands and after managing to cuff a couple, I had to run a gauntlet getting whipped to shit by their buckles, hell I had welt marks all over me for a couple of weeks, bit of a bummer but these things are sent to try us!

I would tend to visit most of the roughest local boozers that were around at that time........The Cock and Bottle, The Old Crown, The Delacey etc. These, amongst plenty of other Bradford pubs, were rough gaffs and you would always see plenty of 'activity' inside and outside of these premises. It was invariably a 'play' on your own safety to visit the toilets in some of these places and in the Beacon pub at Buttershaw, I played the card. I entered the Gents and came across a guy who was headbutting the mirror and shouting "Bastard". "Bastard" ! Blood was pissing from his forehead and he just turned and stared at me. I eyeballed him for a couple of minutes whilst I had my piss and then quickly exited...........you meet all kinds!

Brian had a Kawasaki 250cc bike at this time but all the 'chat' of a big scooter revival was in the air and for him and me, that was the buzz we were after. Off we trotted down to Len's Scooters in Shipley, having a good look round to see what was on offer and what sort of dosh we were going to have to lay out. Brian bought a Vespa and I parted with £300 for a Lambretta GP200, which was metallic silver with metallic purple flames all over it. Looking back, I can't but think that some fucker completely had my pants down with the price I was charged but what goes around comes around and there were a few people who ripped them off later in life……..another story!

The Lambretta looked the dog's bollocks but it was shite really and was forever breaking down, bleeding nightmare! There were a few Scooter clubs around then but the top team were The 'B' Boys, (Bradford Scooter Club), so we headed for The Top House pub at Odsal, where they met, to chance our hands. We were accepted on a month's trial and I was on the books at number 33, a far cry from the top spot but time was on my side. The club was run well, everything formatted, bank account, set times for meetings, fines and you were issued with two cloth badges and one plastic stick on badge after the month's trial. Positions were held in respect of the effort put in, with regard to attendance of meetings, club runs and any other input that was beneficial. The first club run I went on was to Scarborough, which was always the first weekend in November and as I recall, it was pissing down. Football was pushed into the background, although I still was present at some games but this was a completely new buzz for me. Some guys were going for the day and a far few were staying over until the Sunday. It was a poor turn out and there were only around seven that stayed over, even so, we were brawling with the locals before it was dark! Womers was the number one, Winker (who was a scaffolder and had forearms like Popeye) number two and ex number one Jeff Johnno was number three, all were present on that trip. Even though the shitty Lambretta packed up a couple of times on the way home, I earned some 'Brownie' points and moved up to number 25 on the meeting night, the following Thursday.

It was a bit of an elite club and if members didn't fit the criteria, they were soon 'binned'. We always went to Blackpool at Easter, whereas all the other clubs for miles around would always head off to Scarborough and because of this we were pretty much classed as outcasts but what the hell, we had a hard core of top guys and didn't give a monkey's arse. Blackpool was full of bikers over Easter, so we were always going to get some grief but it was never too heavy and when we did get some, we always held our own. We got to the stage where everyone wore an R.A.F great coat, black helmet and more often than not, black Doc Martin boots, we were like a small, well run army unit. The 'B' boys had a well established name and not many other scooter boys would mess much but there were always a few new clubs on the block that didn't quite know the score. One evening, while riding through town, Chaz spotted a scooter with a B.S.C shield on the back, he pulled the kid and asked what club he was in and the lad stated that he was in the Brighouse club. Chaz worked at our place and he'd started going down town with myself and Bri and was instantly into the scooter scene, buying a 'Silver Jubilee' painted Vespa Rally, which was well nice from Dean, another 'B' Boy. Well, we took a team down to their boozer and soon put them straight, there were only one true B.S.C in the area and still are to this day!

Still on the town and having a few rucks here and there with all kinds really, town boys, other scooter lads, punk rockers and bikers. Russ is slightly younger than me, yet I'd known him from school and from around Girlington, probably since I was about 12. He'd bought a Vespa Rally scooter, a beauty, with a 'church glass' windows paintwork on it, I vouched for him and he joined the 'B' Boys, along with, 'Boy' Evens and Zippy (John Kadjersky). John is the most passionate Polish guy I've ever met, a cheeky amusing fucker and all round good bloke. I'd soon bounced up to number 18 then to number 12 and shot straight up to number 5, which annoyed quite a few of the older end that had been in the club a lot longer than I had. When numbers were acquired, you received a large wooden shield, painted in the club colours of black, white and green, with the club name on and your number on the bottom. On the Thursday in question, when I reached number 5, there was a bit of unrest and a few winging that I'd moved up too quick but I never missed any meetings or club runs and I was the one fighting for the club's name every weekend in the town and I recall saying that if any of them had a problem, then the car park was only two seconds away........no takers. Winker had other commitments and wasn't really too bothered about putting the time into the club at that time, so Womer announced me as his number 2 with Chaz edging his way into number 4.

It was at that time that my mate Paul Greig had decided to marry his girlfriend Janet, Dave Moore, who went to school with myself and Paul was supposed to be his best man but pulled out with a couple of days to go, so Greigy asked me to do the honours. I shit myself really but made the effort and managed to get through the day, speeches and all. I remember thinking that standing up and speaking to a couple of hundred people, who were solely transfixed on you and listening to your every word, was the most frightening experience of my life!

After meetings on a Thursday night, we would generally shoot off for some snap or down town for some extra lush. There was a club called Maxims that we frequented and another little back street gaff called Kandy's, which was a few cellars that had been knocked through and converted. Both places were visited by quite a lot of Mods and scooter boys and were always very busy. One Saturday night a few of us were in Kandys and it was pretty busy with 'old' town boys and BCFC Ointment lads. The tunes were belting out and the D.J, Charlie was in his element as the manor rocked, he was later on Crimewatch for a big car swindling scam that supposedly ran off at around £250,000, the lawmen were chasing the wind for about 18 month until they caught up with him!

Anyhow, three blokes came in dressed in suits and looked like they were well oiled; they got beers and stood on the edge of the dance floor. There were a few revellers strutting there stuff on the floor and the 'suits' seemed quite amused with one guy, who was dancing away in a world of his own. The lad was wearing a flat cap, wasn't that big and was minding his own business but the 'suits' were taking the piss and right. There were pillars all over the place that held the structure up and they had little ledges on them where folk placed their drinks. After around ten minutes of the piss taking, the dancing lad suddenly spun round and in one swift movement, grabbed a pint glass from the ledge, smashed it on the pillar and lunged towards one of the suited geezers on the edge of the floor. The glass slashed open the bloke's cheek and then the lad dropped it on the floor and actually carried on dancing for a few seconds, before picking his jacket up and casually walking up the steps and leaving! The chap with the wound just stood there in shock, lifted his hand and touched his teeth through the gaping hole that was now apparent, as the cheek had flapped down, there was blood pouring out all over the place. There was mass panic, people shouting and running around with towels, as everyone began to realise what had happened, I just turned to Chaz and said we'd best be on our toes before the place kicked off or before it was swarming with law.

The other drum we frequented, Maxims, was a lot bigger than Kandys and was on a two floor basis, paying in at ground level and then climbing steps to each floor. This place was always a busy gaff and full of scooter boys and Mod types, with all the latest tunes such as Madness, Secret Affair, Police, Jam, The Beat, as well as all the old SKA and sixties stuff. Myself, Chaz and fat Bri knew plenty of the big town crew that were always in there and we got on sweet with most of them. A kid called Tim Nixon, he also went to Rhodesway and was a year younger than me, he was always around the town and one night we were in there having a few when Tim started arguing with a couple of biker lads in leathers that had made their way in, one thing led to another and Tim was at it with this big, long haired geezer in the middle of the dance floor. His mate spun and squared up with me, swinging big hay makers, well we smartened the pair of them up before the bouncers arrived to split everyone up, no problem, nothing too heavy. Shortly after, me and Chaz decided to see what the skirt situation was like downstairs and as we went through the door, we were confronted by five leather clads, the kid that I'd had the rumble with was at the front and in a breath had me pinned to wall with a blade stuck to the bone right on my chin end.....lovely! His words were "you're not so smart now twat and Ill run this shiv right down to your belly".

I was stuck there, him almost frothing at the mouth and pushing the blade, so that I was on tip toes, this seriously wasn't funny. Luckily, one of the other blokes that was there, was a biker that worked at Renolds and he persuaded the guy to lower the knife, there was a bit of roughing up, a trickle of blood from my chin end and they were gone. Never seen the knife kid again, life is, you live and learn.

I'd mix with the town scooter guys/mods in the Queens pub occasionally and kept up to speed with what was happening in the centre with Meddy, Dave Pickles, Craig Normanton, Bottle to name a few. I was out with Mark, Tim, Donald, Metro and some others one evening and we were parking up in an underground car park in the town, when a large group of bikers arrived giving it large. We were well outnumbered but were tooled up with iron bars, hammers and bats, all located under the scooter seats. The confrontation didn't last long but there was plenty of 'claret' and I've no doubt, a few bones broken before we managed to get out of there.

We had a weekend away from the scootering, as my mate Billy worked as a manager for the coach company, Wallace Arnold and each year they organised a trip to Amsterdam. For the second year in succession, Bill managed to arrange for a few of us to get on the trip, so after an evening on the ale in Leeds, we made our way to the rendezvous and piled onto the coach. Billy, Ian, Russ, Chaz, my brother Pete and myself, were all in high spirits as we made our way down to Dover. The coach had picked up a few pub landlords on the way and each one of them had brought plenty of alcohol with them, so it was a very rowdy trip! Everyone was bollocksed, catching the odd hour of sleep here and there as we made our way through France and Belgium before arriving in Amsterdam. The 'digs' weren't brilliant but were well adequate for a trip full of revellers on the piss for the weekend. There was a guy called Malcolm who owned the Oliver Twist pub at Wakefield and whether we were in the digs or in any boozer, he pulled out a small set of traffic lights and said that as long as the light was green, he was in the chair to pay for whatever us lads were drinking....absolutely top draw. There were a few short trips that had been booked for us to go on, one being a short excursion to a cheese making factory. It was an interesting jaunt and apparently, the Dutch had used the cheese making procedure since the beginning of time. All the representatives of the guided tour wore national dress and as lads do, we started taking the piss and dancing around singing the Madness, Baggy Trousers, which didn't go down too well and we were promptly thrown out! The same thing happened at the clogg making factory and I think the organisers of our trip were growing slightly thin on the patience front. We drove up to Volendam, where there was a large model village site, it was absolutely brilliant, and it was superbly laid out, with a large airport in the centre. Well, at the time there was a TV advert out, I think it was British Airways, with the logo, 'Fly the flag', so we got silly and ran down the runway singing the tune at the tops of our voices, carrying on and knocking over a couple of the planes, just lads really. Our foolishness didn't last long and we were promptly escorted from the site by armed police! We had to find a boozer and wait for the rest of our party to finish their tour of the village. Top bollocks trip though and I would advise anyone that hasn't been to Amsterdam, to give it a go because it's one hell of a place, very cosmopolitan, good bars, great restaurants, legalised drugs, porn in abundance and of course, very picturesque!

There was never a dull night in the town, always something going off, there was a scooter club from Leeds occasionally came over, always crewed up, called the Gemini. One of their guys was called Big Tony Moore (Moore Moore) and one night there was a rumble at the bar in Maxims and he got glassed in the cheek, I recall a guy called Pete Vasey being in the frame for it, he was an Ointment boy and reportedly a bit tasty. Well there was hell to pay, as the Vase had just got a scooter and had visited our crew a few times with Bri. The Gemini came looking for Pete a few times, no probs really, didn't get too far out of hand, a lot of threats and scuffles but no major set too. In the club, there were three brothers, Jeff, Doug and big Jock Johnson, well Doug had a straightener with the Vase outside an ale house after a bit of verbal and Doug smartened him in a breath. I know that the Vase died but I'm not sure whether he had an overdose or died in a crash but he passed on, either way.

Doug was always a bit quick tempered, which didn't go down too well with a lot of our guys but me and him always got on sound and we are still top mates to this day. Jeff was also a handy bloke and 'rested' at number three in the club, it was a position that ex-number one's held, as a mark of respect, he was sound and now lives in Spain, I've seen him on the odd occasion over the years, a good old spunker!! Ha. Jock, real name Steve was like the 'daddy' of the club, a big guy who could drink for England and the rest!! A gentle giant but could do the business if needed, poor guy had an accident down an embankment and died, there were hundreds at the funeral, God rest his soul, a big, big man.

There's a 'walk' called the Lyke Wake Walk which starts in Osmotherley in the North Yorkshire moors and ends in Ravenscar near the East coast. There were some guys that Womers worked with, who were attempting this arduous task for charity. Womers, in his infinite wisdom, thought it would be a good idea for some of us to get involved and prove to people that there was a lot more to us than met the eye! Wom, Chaz and myself decided that we would have no problem in completing the 42 mile hike and with no preparation whatsoever, we 'signed up'.

There were around twenty blokes in our party of walkers and we set off at midnight with the cold Yorkshire wind blowing straight through us. We had regular check points along the way that supplied us with food and drink and any other back-up that was needed. We soon realised that this event wasn't for the fainthearted and there were the odd participant dropping out at each checkpoint either with blistered feet or just unable to carry on. We reached the finish 15 hours later, wet, cold, shattered and with blistered feet but had completed the hard slog nevertheless. We were chuffed to fuck at our accomplishment but I said afterwards that I don't think any of us would ever again attempt something of that magnitude without the proper preparation.

We would always go out on the town if it was one of the lads birthdays and occasionally get into the Mecca on the outskirts of town. In there one Saturday night having a 'ball', top crew, with Womer, Doug, Jeff, Russ, Chaz, Hairy Bob, Parks and a few others. Bob had this big gingerish beard, which he'd had since being about sixteen, something to do with a shaving rash?? Anyhow, he was always a big guy who could drink a fair few beers and always behaved with this 'father' figure aura about him. On the night in question, we'd done the town and were fooling about on the dance floor, not bothering anyone, when this large, fattish bloke spun round and accused Chaz of bumping into him. Womer and Big Bob, in his 'dad' like manor, were trying to calm the situation down and offered to by a few beers, when the fat guy suddenly whacked Chaz straight in the boat race, knocking onto some tables with claret pissing from his snout, game on! Jeff landed a beauty on the guy and no word of a lie, the stone out of his ring, was stuck in his forehead!! The piece of Onyx didn't deter him and along with his mates, he waded into anyone that was near him. The dance floor pretty much emptied quite quickly and we were having a right set too, with extra acquaintances of the fat guy, running on from all directions. There were bodies laid out on the floor and blood all over the place, with the fat bloke eventually hitting the deck, after being overpowered by Doug and the hairy one. The doormen didn't appear until they had the law to back them up, which was our cue to mingle in with all the other punters that were packed around the dance floor. Now getting out of the place was in a situation like that was an art in itself, our guys were getting lifted left, right and centre and I was trying to lose myself in the crowds. I moved in and out of punters and tried to reach an exit but all seemed to be covered by lawmen or door staff. I managed to reach the steps which led to the main entrance but as I started to 'leg' it up the stairs, a big burly copper flattened me and smashed me, head first into the steps. He said that he'd noticed me because the white trousers I had on were covered in claret all over the bottoms and with that, he led me into the manager's office. The office was full of our chaps and a few uniforms and I was the last of the bunch to be pulled in, ready to be levelled by the top brass lawman that who was sat in the 'big' chair. He said that there were a few hospital casualties and we would all be getting dragged down town for the night to face the consequences. A minute later, another officer came in and the top man went outside with him for a chin wag. On his return, he said that three women who had been sat near the dance floor had seen most of the incident and were insistent that we were not blame for the 'kick off' at all, so with that, he said that no changes would be made and we were all free to go but must leave the premises immediately. Womer was as arrogant as ever and asked if we could have our entrance money refunded, seeing as we'd only been in the place for half an hour, which, of course, went down well! A good curry was the end to that eventful evening but not before the fat geezer with the Onyx stone stuck in his forehead, had passed us in a taxi, shouting and bawling and calling us all wankers ……..weird guy!

Russ was covering a Milk Round for a relation named Andy and asked me to give him a hand and also make a few quid…no probs. One night though, we'd been out for a beer with Varley and on the way back to the farm I lost Russ and ended up on my scooter riding towards Clayton. It was raining heavily when suddenly the road 'disappeared' and I tried to squeeze down the side of a motor to avoid a bad smash. Unfortunately I clipped the curb, ended up going arse over tit over the handlebars and hitting a wire fence around five foot from the ground, completely upside down! I landed in a crumpled heap on the deck but after shaking myself down, I managed to restart the 'chariot' and eventually arrived at the farm. After delivering the milk a few hours later, I was on my way to work to do a full shift and there were a few bits of 'Vespa' left on the road in my wake!!! I had obviously smashed with slightly more impact than I thought!

Christmas was always a time for fancy dress and all our guys were in the frame for a good laugh where that was concerned. The week before Christmas in 1980, we'd hired a room at the back of the Bowling Hotel pub for a do, with plenty of food on, a DJ and so on. Absolutely top do, Russ turned up as the Phantom Flan Flinger (from the TV programme, Tiswas), Dean Halmshaw was a good Grim Reaper and everyone else was all on the same level with their costumes. Towards the end of the night, we decided to hit town, as we'd heard of one or two other 'do's' that were going on. There was a wine bar at the bottom end of Bradford town centre called Bonaparte's and we all headed for that with most of our other halves in tow. The place was heaving, with everyone in fancy dress, no problem, the doorman welcomed us all in and I pushed my way through to the bar. I was dressed as the Ayatollah Khomeini and had this 'top draw' beard on, my auntie Jean, God bless her, had done it for me and it was made up of all these individual bits of hair that were all stuck on.....looked great....... to start with! Sue, my girlfriend of the time, was dressed as Little Bow Peep and as I was trying to get served, she was a few yards way near the bar. there was hardly enough room to turn and the bloke behind her, who was dressed as a Quaker, was openly fondling her and after me giving a round of threatening 'fucks', he made some gesture and told me to shut the fuck up. Well, after pushing a through a few people, my cigarette ended up in his cheek, the scuffle ended up with us both outside but unbeknown to me, he knew the doorman and a couple of his mates followed us out, one dressed as a baseball guy, with a bat and the other dressed as a Viking, with some kind of wooden staff, great! So I am, in a cull-de-sac with the Quaker running straight at me, no probs there, I managed to drop him on his arse, just as Womer, dressed as a Gorilla, came falling through the door. All five of us were at it, full whack with me and Wom holding our own, not bad really, to say that we were getting a few cracks from their tools. Within minutes, the bouncer had let another half dozen of their crew out and the two of us were getting a right pasting. Our guys managed to give the doorman a roughing up and come to our assistance, good job because we were more or less out of the game by then but the tide turned. The law weren't far away and there were bodies, all in fancy dress, legging it in all directions, as they arrived. Poor Womers bollocks were up around his ears, so he was well out of it really and myself, Sue, Winker, Russ and Chaz headed through town to get a cab. Near the taxi rank, the Quaker and his two mates showed up again and another rook was in motion, this time, we were well on top but the law turned up and the three of them were arrested, along with Myself, Chaz and Winker. Next morning, we were all kicked out of the back door of the nick at different times; the main problem for me was that it was around 8.30am, I had no pockets, so no dosh and the pillocks wouldn't let me make a phone call. I had to leg it across town in the morning rush hour, covered in cuts and bruises and looking a total twat in that fancy dress outfit, find a phone box, reverse the charges and get my 'old Queen' to come and pick me up.....tremendous! over the next two or three months, we were in and out of court, half a dozen times, as the other geezers were in the Army and never showed up, due to various excuses. I was eventually bound over to keep the peace for twelve months, not much chance of that then.

Still hitting the footie when time permitted, if there was no scooter runs arranged. One away trip to Tottenham Hotspur saw an absolute tragedy occur, where a young lad, who worked with us in the engineering, was murdered in an ambush attack on the way up to the ground. There were a coach load of us Bradford Whites walking up the main road and there were two large pubs, about a hundred yards apart, both were occupied by the Spurs fans. When we were between the two, fans came running out of them both and cut off our exits, the result being total mayhem with fists and boots flying everywhere. The majority managed to get through and up the road but one or two were left battered and poor young Jeremy Burton was on the pavement edge and consequently died. Tragic.....young Jeremy was a nice young kid and should never have been taken at such an early age.

In the May of 1981, five of us 'B Boys' were on the lash one Saturday night in Bradford, we'd been round the town in all the 'old' boozers, such as the Boy and Barrel, Lord Clyde, Packhorse and a few other drums, before ending up in a night club called Annabella's. Not a bad gaff, some good tunes and always reasonably busy, we ordered some ales and Wom, Boy Berwyn and Fern headed for the dance floor, whilst myself and Chaz looked for some seats. There a few seats quite near the bar, two Asian kids and a black guy were sat round two tables and then there was one Asian kid, sat on his own, close to them but taking up a further two small tables. I asked the lad to move up and let us sit down but he just sat there staring at us and made no movement or reply, I asked him again but got the same response, so I told the prick to move his shitty arse! He moved and we sat down and started chatting but from our left, all we were getting, was "white bastards, who do you think you are", then it was "you don't know who you're messing with, we're boxers and we'll knock fuck out you". It was obvious that it was going to get physical and as they stood up Chaz and I were into them in a breath. I was then hit with a pint glass just underneath the eye and got wedged in between two tables, the guy was on top of me and to save myself from having being fully glassed, my only option was to stick a thumb straight in the guy's eye, hence I was soon back on my feet. The other three in our team were there in a breath and shortly after, the 'boxers' were all on the deck covered in claret. They might have been ok in a ring but were definitely no match for boots, elbows and foreheads! I'd have topped myself if I'd been training those 'so called' boxers, they were fucking useless bastards and hit like a bunch of fucking women! The doormen were well stand offish and were trying the "calm down lads" approach, rather than getting to grips with us, so after a bit of a stand off, we were outside on the cobbles under our own steam but shortly after that, we were pinched and down the cells getting charged. We had no joy in the Plod house, it was as one sided as an early Mike Tyson fight! In the custody room, a short Irish copper was playing the big, I am type, he threw his cap across the room and I had to quickly shift so it didn't hit me in the 'boat'. He kept slating us and asking if any of us fancied our chances with him, well out of order, seeing as he knew none of us could actually stand up and have a dig with him and get away with it. A couple of hours later, when I was all drowsy and had been dozing on and off, I was pulled out for questioning and the short plod was pushing me down the corridor, still 'chelping' on that it was pricks like us that made his job hard. Why is it that most of the short folk of this world seem to feel hard done by with regard to their size and think that the rest of us owe them something? If any of them grab any sort of power position, they tend to think that they have more to prove than the rest of us and turn out to be complete arseholes!! Anyway, out on bail the next day and that was my binding over order well shagged. We were charged with various assaults, wounding and affray, so with that little lot, we were in and out of court for a couple of month until they adjourned it to Crown court later in the year.

Late into work again the next day, the bloke who ran the department that I worked in then, was a chap called Eric Lancaster, he was a sound guy and I had to nip in and explain to him what had happened. He said I was young and foolish and all the scrapping and confrontations would be something that I would grow out of. His second in command was a right prat of a foreman called Pullein and was always at logger heads with everyone as he tried to impose his authority. The amount of times that tools went down and the fitting section that I worked in, walked out, was unbelievable. We would be across the road in the pub for an hour, before Lancaster sent someone across to ask everyone to come back and get things sorted out. Pullein would never apologise for his actions and continued to fuck up situations and annoy numerous members of the workforce on a daily basis, occasionally though, he'd come down off his high horse and was actually quite human!! Once, after he and I had a full blown 'verbal' over 'piece work' times, I recall him saying that engineers like me were ten a penny. I told him that it was engineers like me that kept shitheads like him in a job and that if I ever came across him in the 'ale house', I'd sit him straight on his daft arse!!

Chapter 6

To the north of the Dales is a great village called Hawes. This place was a good haunt for us when away for a weekend of camping, there's a boozer called the Green Dragon, set a couple of mile or so outside the village, on the way up to the 'falls' and quite a few times, we camped on land at the back of it. We'd been on the lash one afternoon and made our way up to the Dragon to camp, a good ten of us on the scoots and big Ducka in his Escort car and Chaz in a small van. Well, the tents were being pitched and there was plenty of banter going around, when Ducka decides to take a piss at the back of the two motors but instead of leaking on the grass, he pissed on one of the wheels of Chaz's van! Chaz went ballistic, shouting and bawling at the Duck, saying he was the filthiest bastard he'd ever met but Ducka was unmoved and said it was only a bit of unwanted ale that would come off if it rained.

Into the Dragon for a quick bar meal and a couple of swift 'jars', then it was decided we would head into the village and see what the North Yorkshire people's hospitality was offering. Myself, Chaz and Womer decided to cut across the river to save the walk round the winding country roads and of course, to get to the ale house first! The main pub was really busy, full of guys and there were a few families and couples sat outside on the large forecourt. We'd got a beer each and were stood on the steps of the pub, still dripping wet from the waist down, when Ducka arrived on someone's scooter. For some reason, Womer had his car keys and he wanted them, so he could drive Jeff down to the village (Jeff had a broken leg at the time and was in plaster). With the keys in his possession, the Duck drove off but as he did so, one of the guys in the boozer stood next to us on the pub steps and started shouting "scooter wanker" and a load of other old shite. Womer, straight in, poured his pint over the blokes head and told him to shut the fuck up, as the Duck was with us. The bloke started screaming and ran into the boozer, shouting at the top of his voice, "we're chewing lads!". The three of us moved off the steps and on the forecourt, as 24 Geordies came piling out to confront us, we were obviously in a bit of shit at that point. A big bearded bloke walked over and said that it would be in our best interest to move on to one of the other pubs, well, Womer just looked at me and Chaz and told the guy to get fucked off. Another, older bloke then walked over, basically telling us the same, saying it was a pointless stand we were making and that we would definitely regret our actions, same reply. A long haired, scruffy looking pillock started shouting the odds as he came towards us and was pointing at Womer saying we were going to get a knacking. He was a metre away looking straight at Wom, when he suddenly spun and butted me, smashing my nose, sending me reeling backwards. Wom decked him with a left hook and the next thing I knew, I was getting showered in pint glasses, followed by a rake of fists and boots, sure enough, we were getting a bit of a bashing! Chaz was pinned to a car bonnet by the big bearded guy and his mate, I was trying to cover up best I could but copped for plenty and

Womer was underneath a dozen sets of size nines and tens! The hiding stopped quite abruptly when a few of the Geordies tried to call a halt to the kicking and they started throwing punches at each other. Myself and Chaz managed to pull Wom out of the firing line and we were licking our wounds, when the rest of our lot turned up, as kids and women were legging it away from the forecourt. I had little cuts down my face, neck and forearms where the glasses had hit me, a fat lip and a few other cuts and bruise, nothing major but Wom was struggling a bit, after being booted in the 'plums' half a dozen times. Jeff, limping about with his cast on, decided it was in our best interest to smarten ourselves up in one of the other ale houses further down the road. Half hour later our Geordie 'friends' came poling in but as we got ready for a square up, most of them were apologising and getting rounds of beers in, saying they had loads of respect for us, for standing our ground and didn't want any more confrontation. One or two of them were still quite smart about it but the rest of their guys put them in their place. Later, a few of the Geordie guys said they were having a bit of a 'do' up the road, where they were camped and said we were welcome to come up for beers and a bit of a barbeque. I'd pulled a local skirt, so I was up for it and the Duck and a couple more also fancied it but the majority of our guys said fuck em and headed back towards the Dragon. It was a decent bash up at their camp, with quite a few local birds in the frame but as the ale flowed in abundance, one or two of their lot started getting a bit too leery for our liking, so it was time to move on. I took the local lass home and an hour or so later, I ended up at the back of the Dragon, to find our guys, fire blazing and plenty of tins passing hands. Chaz was out for revenge for Ducka's pissing antics earlier, so he squat down on the Ducks car bonnet and deposited a rather large, sloppy turd! Well, we howled with drunken laughter and after a few more tins, it was time to get our heads down. Next morning, the Duck came across this mess on his Escort bonnet and hit the clouds, calling Chaz the dirtiest scumbag on God's earth and he then picked up the nearest thing to hand and proceeded to wipe the shit off the motor. Only thing was that he'd actually picked up fat Bri's Bradford City scarf, which by this time, was blathered in the stinking stuff!! Bri's turn to throw a double six, he and the Duck were almost toe to toe and had to be kept apart, the shit had certainly hit the fan.

Another place in the Dales that we visited a lot, was Hubberholme, near Buckden, great little place that was made up of one pub called the George, a church and a bridge, a quality, quiet little serene place. We were usually lucky enough to have a motor in tow when we went on camping 'runs', which were great for filling up with all the tents and the rest of the gear and leaving the scooters, a lot easier to handle down the winding country lanes. All tents pitched, gear sorted, then into the George for some lubrication, the boozer wasn't very big, quite dingy really but it had a friendly atmosphere and on an evening, there was usually always someone playing guitars, flutes or some other folk type instruments. On the end of the bar, there was always a large candle burning and I once made the major mistake of blowing it out......oops! The bar was instantly closed and I was the biggest twat in the world according to almost everyone in the gaff but after pleading my innocence and ignorance, the bar was reopened, which

I think may have saved me from a lynching. When the candle's alight, the bar's open and when it's out, the bar's shut, pretty simple really, even for a gang of loony scooter boys. Most ale houses stuck to the standard opening times in those days, so come three in the afternoon, we'd usually play football and with the club numbers, it was always odd numbers verses evens, with any 'extra' guys we had with us, split between. You had to have your wits about you with the B.Boy rules because one minute, you'd be running along with the ball and the next, you were pole axed from a forearm smash.........play on! Some great games were had and after every game, there were always photo's taken of both winning and losing teams. Someone would be delegated for cooking duties, so once all had been fed and watered; it was back to the boozer for a good old sing song and knees up. We met a couple of guys that were camping at the other side of Hubberholme, decent pair, that could down plenty of 'lush' and were up for a good laugh, these blokes were Welsh (poor pillocks). When we were all bundled out the ale house, we decided to get a large fire going in the field where we were camped and to everyone's amazement, these two Welsh head cases were straight into the river tooled up with big knives! Hence, it wasn't long before we were all eating red hot duck before hitting the sack. Scooter runs like those were always top draw and a good laugh but nothing compares on a laughter scale as the 'Hairy Bob' incident, as I call it. Womer had stepped down and I was now the head 'poncho', we'd set off on Friday teatime, more or less straight from work and was absolutely pissing it down, as we headed for Aysgarth, not too far from Hawes. This was one of the 'mixed' runs, so most of us had our other halves with us and on reaching the outskirts of Aysgarth, we nipped straight into a biggish boozer and out of the rain. The landlord was sound and had no problem with us all piling in, so straight away it was a club 'round' (out of the club savings) for the drinks. We all had a few beers and some grub and the landlord said he had a field at the back where we could get camped, so before it got too dark, we decided to venture out into the rain and get sorted. There was a short track to the gate and then a very steep 'tractor' track down to a quite flat field at the bottom. The rain was still coming down heavy and one or two managed to get down before Hairy Bob made his attempt, well, he started skidding and sliding down the track, his front wheel got wedged in the mud and he went arse over tit. The big man ended up in a heap at the bottom of the track with his scooter half on top of him, he jump up, yellow over trousers, RAF coat and beard all covered in thick mud and tried to act like nothing had happened but the rest of us were in total hysterics, unless you'd been there, you can't possibly appreciate how hilarious it was, I still snigger at the thought. Tents pitched, all back into the boozer and another top weekend was had by all.

Our badges were (and still are!) a part of a 'B Boys' body, so there was hell to pay if any went missing or if anyone was putting it about that they were in possession of one. We never gave any away or sold any and we never wore any other badges apart from our own. One Thursday evening I went down to the Salthorn pub for the meeting and sent Russ, my number 2, down to a boozer in town, along with Bob, Jeff and Fearn, to another club's meeting to have a 'word' with a guy who'd been putting it about that he had one of our badges. Russ rang the Satlhorn when they'd arrived (no mobiles in those days!) and said that there were around thirty five guys there and the bloke in question had denied he'd said it and that he'd never had one of the badges in his possession at all. Well, he got one of Russ's slaps for wasting our time, none of their guys questioned the action, in fear of any major repercussions and our lads arrived at our meeting pub around twenty minutes later. The incident was never heard about again. Russ had earned the nickname 'One punch' after an incident outside Kandys one night. There had been a large group of skinheads kicking off in the centre of Bradford and a few of them had chased a couple of guys into Kandys club, unaware that the place was full of 'lads'. We had a ruck on the cobbles outside with their mob and as they 'legged' it, half of them well battered and bashed, Russ decked their main guy with a single big right hander! Quality to watch.

As I've mentioned, we never really mixed with many other scooter clubs and went our own way but there was a National run to the Isle of Man and we decided to make one in on that. Great turn out; we had levelled out at around twenty members, all good, solid lads and were set for a top weekend across the water. Over to Heysham, near Morecombe on the Friday night and found ourselves a decent ale house for a few jars before it was time to make our way down to the ferry. Not much sleep on the ferry, plenty of beers and a few quid won in the 'casino'. It was a bit foggy, as I recall when we docked at Douglas on the Isle of Man and as we we'd all had 'plenty', we had to be careful driving into the docking area. There were plenty of scooter guys everywhere, so we knew it wouldn't be easy finding digs, so it was breakfast first and then send four 'scouts' out in different directions to see what they could come up with. They were all back within the agreed hour and luckily for us there was a large boarding house, not too far away, that could accommodate us all. We checked in with the landlord, who was actually a tad round the bleeding bend but we could put up with that, heads down for some well earned shut eye before lunch. We were all up and about around midday and after some snap and a few ales, we decided to catch some 'rays' in a park, which had an idyllic little lake with boats and such, you can picture the scene. The decision was, to have a bit of a laze and a bit of rowing but after ten minutes or so of that, things went pear shaped. It only took one collision or one splash and it was a full on war with all the bloody boats being soaked and half the lads almost being drowned, as we all took sides. The poor old 'dear', who was in charge of the boat hire, was going mental and it wasn't long before we saw sense and dragged all the boats to shore, emptied them and left the place as we'd found it, quite a good laugh for other punters that were either waiting to get on or who were already on the lake but well out of harms way.

We had a quality weekend, involved in a couple of skirmishes but without really getting in any bother (for a change), all our scooters were kicked over on the second night but we expected something like that, as it was the T.T. biking event, the weekend after, so there were a few 'early' leather clads there but they kept well in the 'shade', so to speak. There was a bit of a 'rally' on the Sunday morning, there were roughly around 600 scooter lads who had made the trip, so it was once right round the island, quite impressive to watch.

The West Riding Scooter club, another club based in Bradford, organised a photo shoot, with all the Bradford and surrounding area clubs, with a magazine called Scooterama. It took place on a Sunday lunchtime outside a big boozer called The Furnace, on Halifax Road on the outskirts of Bradford, where the West Riding club had their meetings. When we arrived, there were already quite a few clubs there, the Red Lion, from Heckmondwyke, Road Runners, from Shipley, West Riding, Night Owls and one or two others. They were all positioning there bikes for the shoot but we pulled rank as THE Bradford scooter club and took centre stage, the photographer was across the road, getting as wide a shot as he could and this was causing havoc with the traffic. The pictures were a total success, well for us anyway, we had the centre section and on the front page of the magazine, there were just half a dozen other scoots, apart from B Boys. We mixed with some of the West Riding guys that afternoon, down on grassland in the estate, music blasting and plenty of beers, the organiser was a bloke called Dermott Nash, who was 'acting' number one for the West Riding at the time, good day.

We generally got on with West Riding guys but there were always a few that were jealous to fuck of us and used to slate us off at any opportunity. A guy called Molly Morrell was their main number one and he was never keen on any of our lot and still isn't to this day. One Saturday night I was going down town with Chaz and Russ and my brother Pete was at a lose end and asked if he could make one in with us, no probs. We'd had a half decent night in the town and ended up at Kandy's night club, which as usual, was pretty packed.

I was stood chatting with Russ and Chaz, when there was a bit of a rumpus at the bar and on looking over, I noticed it was our Pete in the centre of the disturbance. Apparently, he'd been chatting with Molly's missus, which, obviously hadn't gone down too well, as Molly was going to give him a spank. There were twenty or more of his crew there and the long and the short of it was that myself and Molly decided to sort it on the cobbles, one on one. I stood in the middle of the road and waited for him to make his move, the whole club was outside, around 200 punters, a few town boys and a good dozen or so 'Ointment' guys, some of who I knew to talk to. Well, The Moll came into the road saying that I would have to take the brunt for my bro, 'sound' I thought, "bring it on", just then, his missus came running out shouting and bawling about all kinds and he ended up clipping her to shut her up. There's the source of the problem, I thought and shrugged my shoulders, he grabbed hold of her and dragged her back inside, game over, or so I figured. One of the 'Ointment' guys shouted to me that there was another guy saying I was going to cop it and as I looked down the street, a stocky guy, no shirt on and covered in tats, was stood with a chair leg, shouting that he'd smarten me up in a breath. I stood back in the middle of the road and shouted to him to crack on but as soon as I started to run at him, he dropped the weapon and bottled it. Off for a curry then and later, dropped Brother Pete off without a scratch, thank God, ma would have ape otherwise.

Russ was assigned the task of sorting out a weekend away at a place called Bredbury Hall and Country club in Stockport. It was a large manner and quite well to do, apparently they'd turned away George Best a few weeks previous, so we thought we would struggle to get booked in. We turned up on the Friday evening and as we walked through the main entrance, the staff just stood there in awe. Full credit to Russ, he'd booked us in as some kind of business party and after he'd given them plenty of patter at the desk, we were shown to our rooms. When we came down to the bar, which was adjacent to the club area, a couple of bouncers were there issuing us all with plasters to cover up any tattoos and earrings, talk about working to the book. The place was massive; there were around seven different dance floors all playing different types of music. A really busy gaff, with plenty of 'totti', we managed to get through the weekend without getting into any real bother, although the law did arrive after some bird had said her handbag had been nicked, it turned out that she had just left it in one of our lads rooms! Zip was definitely the star of the weekend and even did his own rendition of 'The Devil Went Down To Georgia' by the Charlie Daniels Band, brilliant... that Zip's a legend.

Late that summer, I got engaged to Sue, she was living in a flat at Shelf, just outside Bradford and I was more or less residing there myself. Don't think her dad was too keen about Sue getting engaged to a skinheaded scooter boy who was always rucking and who was full of himself but the rest of her family seemed suited. The unfortunate thing was that the court case over the night club incident was on its way and it wasn't looking too good. Just to put the icing on the cake, a few of us were in the Salthorn pub playing pool one Saturday dinnertime and then decided to nip up to one of the lads houses when we'd done. Driving on a country lane just further down the road, we came to a halt, as three bikes were blocking the road. I couldn't get passed on the narrow road and one of the bikes set off and banged into the side of me, no apology or anything, as this happened, I kicked the bike over and the rider couldn't hold up the big beast and fell over. The next thing a big bearded, leather clad hoogie came up from behind and belted me right in the side of the boat race, knocking me off the scoot onto the road. I struggled to get from underneath the vehicle as he came at me for a second shot but managed to roll away and get to my feet. Punches were thrown and I collared him in a head lock, which brought his helmet off and as he came at me again, I swung the helmet and connected full on, knocking him clean off his feet. Well that was that, I lost my temper and gave it to the prat for assaulting me and starting the rook in the first place. His mates had got roughed up in the road and people were running out of the pub to try and get to the bottom of what was going on. We left the scene and to be honest, thought that they'd got what they deserved for starting what should never have happened, what I didn't know, was that the landlady from the pub had taken my scooter registration. Next morning, I was washing the scooter in the driveway at my mom's, sporting a nice big bruise on the cheek, when this guy walked up and started chatting about my vehicle, making out he was really interested in scooters. When I noticed the panda motor rolling across the bottom of the drive, I soon realised who he was and what he was there for. He said he'd just come down from the Infirmary hospital and the big bearded meathead was in there with plenty of facial damage and busted ribs, then asked me if I wanted to get a jacket because after questioning down the nick, I would probably be up before the Beak the following morning, great. Down the slammer I told him the score and explained to him what had happened and he said that the geezer had admitted assaulting me first but seeing as I wasn't the one laid up in the hospital bed, I was lumbered……..charged with ABH again! The next morning I was first up in the Crown court and the judge just adjourned the case and said that they would tag it on to the rest of my charges

CHAPTER 7

Monday, October 19th 1981, the day of reckoning, Leeds Crown Court and a busy, overcast day that started a week I'll never forget. Chaz, Fearn, Womer, Berwyn and myself, all up for the trial for the night club incident and also for myself, was the breaking of the binding over and the spanking of the wannabe hardman biker. We got the train from Bradford to Leeds, and then nipped into a café for bacon butties and a brew, before making our way through the city centre and up to the Crown court. The lads were in good spirits really and the overall opinion was that we were going to get levelled but would probably all be home at the end of the trial. The truth be known, I wasn't that optimistic myself, I had plenty of shit stuck to me and there were riots up and down the country, Leeds, Liverpool, Brixton and the odd kick off in Bradford but nothing major.

The trial was headed by Judge Pickles, not really famous for his leniency throughout the criminal fraternity and as soon as the jury were sworn in and it was duly noted that our identities were rubber stamped, he commented that we would not be allowed to leave the court for lunch, in case we frequented any of the local public houses. Our briefs seemed quite optimistic at the start of the trial and were talking about suspended sentences being the worst scenario, so we were all in reasonable spirits.

The courtroom was packed and the judge had his head down most of the time, as though he wasn't interested in the trial at all and didn't really want to be there....... he probably didn't! Then again, neither did any of us! The doorstaff from the night club, were all sat with the 'boxers' and seemed to be having a good old laugh, all pally like, it sure looked like we were going to get shit on and right. One of the Asians was in the dock and he was looking all round the ceiling and kept screwing his face up and stuttering like Ronnie Barker in 'Open all hours', appeared quite punch drunk to me, crikey, me and Chaz were pissing ourselves and the screws kept telling us to shut the fuck up, or we'd get nailed. The boxers all had their say and were coming out with some right shite, they all said that none of them drank alcohol because they were athletes and it was against their religion. What a load of crap, they were drinking lager and it was a barrel shaped beer glass with a handle on that the clown hit me with. There were flaws in their testimonies when they were cross examined and they contradicted themselves, more than once. The doormen also came out with some right shite, in statements, they made out that they'd seen a hell of a lot more than they could have possibly done, we were getting stitched and not much we could do really. The scooter club was brought up quite a few times and references, as to the way we ran it, were made, it was implied that we had our own little army and were always up for confrontations with anyone who cared to stand in our way. At lunch times, we were down stairs in the cells with a few poxy sandwiches and a pot of tea, the screws were fine with us at that time, chatting away about the trial and our chances and also, chatting about football and other current events etc.

After a couple of days of all out attack from the prosecution, it was the turn of our two Barristers to earn their corn and although they were pretty much on the ball with most facts, there was a sense of a final push missing. I kept thinking that because we had secured Legal Aid, those two Barristers were going to get paid either way and most of the time, seemed to be just going through the motions. There was a real reluctance to even imply that any of the prosecution witnesses were lying, let alone come straight out with it and call them fucking liars! We were on a hiding to nothing and seeing as I'd already dropped myself in the crap over the biker incident, it was nailed on that I was going to get fucked for that. The jury looked a decent bunch really but that can always be deceiving, I always tend to think that half of them are thinking about what they're going to having for their evening meal, rather than concentrating on the facts of the trial that could change some poor fucker's whole life.

Thursday morning, 22nd October 1981 and as on the previous three mornings, we arrived in Leeds city centre and into the café for a spot of breakfast, before making our way up to the court. The atmosphere was more subdued that morning and none of us were really looking forward to standing before Pickles because of the obvious worst scenario. The prosecution put their case forward and then our two Barristers went through the motions, which to be quite honest, left our lads all looking at each other, thinking we were heading for the gallows. Old Pickles did his fancy summing up bit and basically told the jury that we were wrong 'uns and to do the right thing, that was that then, the jury was out and we were again, down the steps into the cells. Lunch time came and went and the jury were still deliberating over whether or not to 'hang' us. Around 3pm, we were lead back up into the courtroom and the jury returned, they'd reached their verdict and we were found guilty on all charges, much to the joy of everyone connected to the prosecution, tremendous! When Old Pickles had decided our fates, Chaz and Fern got 6 months each at a Detention Centre gaff called Gringley, as they were both under 21, Berwyn got sent to Borstal, Womer got a rake of community service hours and I got 6 month for the night club do and 6 month for the biker bloke, brilliant! Pickles said that it appeared to him, that at the slightest hint of any bother, I was the ring leader of a well organised gang of scooter thugs that raised their fists at the drop of a hat and it was best for all if I was taken out of public circulation. With that, apart from Wom, we were taken out of that courtroom and down to those cells for the last time.

We were stripped of our valuables and dumped in separate cells, left to ponder on our predicament, the attitude of the screws had turned 360 and the pally pally side of them had totally disappeared. Our two Barristers came down and chatted to us individually regarding our sentences but the change in their attitudes was also very apparent. I was told that there was no point of appealing against the sentence and that it wasn't that bad considering the charges against me, slightly different outlook to what they'd had a day or two earlier, when they were talking of suspended sentences being the worst option. Obviously, job done, never mind the result, take the money and let these lads take it on the chin....... cheers guys!

Fearn and Chaz were shipped off to the Gringley manor and myself and Berwyn were ushered onto the bus to Armley jail. On arrival at the 'big house', stripped, showered, dressed in shite clobber that didn't even fit and thrown in a totally different world. I sat there in the cell, with a shirt that had half the buttons missing, the fly zip on the trousers was bust and the shoes, although the same size, were different bloody styles, what a shit day this had turned out to be! Berwyn was shipped out to a Borstal and I was stuck in a cell with two other guys, 23 hours a day for the next two and a half weeks, absolutely bored shitless. When the cell door was opened in the morning, it was a mad rush to reach the 'recess' area, with the 'three in a cell' boys, one had a jug for the hot water, one for the cold and the third had the piss bucket. It was chaotic and one morning just as my queue reached the recess opening, some bloke landed a piss bucket right on the back of a guy's napper who was filling his jug. Claret all over the place and the guy, out for the count, fill the jug and move your arse or be stood there looking docile and get pulled in by the screws.

Papers were all sorted and I moved out to Wymott in Leyland, Lancashire that was a place where a tannoy system was set up throughout and you had a key to the cell, although there were certain keys that fit more than one lock and bearing in mind, this was a bloody jail that was half full of thieves! Everybody had to work at that nick, I had a job in the 'Engineers' shop, tapping threads in conduit boxes, did my tree in and so did the next job, which was making metal coat hangers! Hell fire! Had a four jig table and had to produce 4,500 of those bloody things a week, crikey, enough to make anybody go round the damn bend. Eventually, I managed to get a job in the welding section that involved welding up all the base section of the parcel carriers that were used on the railway station platforms. Had to produce a couple of them a day and there was a bit of variation involved in the job, so it wasn't that too bad really. Some weeks, even managed to do a bit of welding on Saturday mornings, which got you out of doing designated cleaning jobs around the landings.

Everyone has their own way of doing their time, for me, it was a case of keeping as busy as possible and not sitting brooding over where you were or why you'd been unfortunate enough to have been sent there in the first place. I would play football, rugby, go out for a run or get down to the gym, whatever was available at the time really. At lock up times, I'd have the radio on and would probably be doing some kind of modelling or a bit of reading, anything to get through the time without pondering about life on the outside. Sue would write to me all the time and would come and visit me every fortnight, we would schedule the visits for Sundays, so in the mornings I would make sure my shirt and trousers were spic and span and try and look reasonably smart.. I was over the moon when she walked into the visiting area but when they called time, it would knock the arse clean out of me and I was always on a bit of a downer for a couple of hours after. The screws always seemed to enjoy calling a halt to the visits and had big smirks all over their faces when they searched you, both before and after you entered the visit. It was always said that the cons were there for a fixed period of time but the screws were there for a lifetime and that would really wind those nice chappies up!

On an evening there was always access to T.V rooms, on each landing there was an I.T.V room and a B.B.C room but occasionally, you'd get some total prick coming in and changing the channel, which more often that not, ended up with someone getting a right spanking, of course, no-one ever saw a thing. Bird was never my cup of tea, the majority of 'cons' where I was, had all done time before, Young Institutions, Borstals, whatever and wherever had no relevance to me, half these guys couldn't hack it on the outside and were quite at home when they were back in 'lock up'. Most of the time, I kept myself to myself but there a few blokes that I got on fine with and ran up a friendship with a few guys. Everybody had their own currency, quite a lot used tobacco, some would use models, others had new 'clobber' form the laundry or the tailors work shop and quite a lot were in the drug business. Drugs were always in abundance, if you were that way inclined, you could lay your hands on pretty much anything you required, it's the way of the world and you have to appreciate that a lot of these 'cons' were convicted for dealing the stuff on civi street.

I spent a bit of time doing modelling and turned out to be a bit of a dab hand at it really, making all kinds of things. At the time you could actually purchase a small craft knife, which was great until some clown stuck one into another inmate's neck! Apparently, the victim went into this guy's cell shouting and bawling about a few bob that was owed and because the guy didn't have the dosh, he smashed up a windmill that the bloke had made from matches. In retaliation, the inmate jumped up and shived him in the throat with the craft knife, well, the moral being there was not to underestimate your opponent! All those little knives were recalled and inmates had to improvise with the aid of razor blades. All inmates in that nick were issued with a new razor blade each week, which seemed absolutely ludicrous to me but that was the system.....barmy really. On return of the used shaving blade, cons used to throw a half blade in the 'pot' and keep half, which could be used to model with or whatever with! The lads that were modelling would stick two matches on each side of the blade and use it as a small knife or serrate the edge and use it as a small saw....clever. A fanatical skinhead from Keighley called Ricky Lister was on our landing, a thief by nature but not a bad lad really, we got on sound and instead of playing the jail barber, who was really just a guy who was given the job and who had probably never cut anybody's hair in his life before doing time, we would sew a razor blade a mm from the edge of a comb and just comb-cut off any excess each day. There were quite a few Bradford lads in there, Bob Murtagh, Russell Holmes, his brother Paddy, just to name a few. There were also quite a few 'baldies' in there at that time and there was always plenty of verbal from the 'long hairs', often resulting in a few straighteners but more shouting matches than 'owt else. One young lad who'd arrived from Strangeways was a typical skinhead livewire with 'skins' and 'Madness' tattoos on his neck, yet he'd been put in his place in the 'nick' over the Pennines. He'd had an altercation with some Jamaican guys and ended up sliced from his arse neck to his arse with a razor blade. He was still trying to put it about in Wymott though.

I played football and rugby for the wing of the nick that I was on, which was good for fitness and was also a great time passer. There was always a set to on the field of play, cons would let off steam and knock fuck out of each other, generally without getting nicked for it, the ref was always a screw and more often than not, he would put the incidents down to frustration and just send the offenders off the field. Occasionally these incidents were carried on later, out of the view of the screws, on the landings or in the landing recesses. One Sunday afternoon, I was on the end of our landing having a smoke and a chat with another inmate from Bradford, called Andy Brough, he was a sound guy and was in for nicking articulated lorries, which I believe was really profitable, until he got nicked of course! Anyway, there was always a kid on the end of the landing, set up as a look out, to make sure there was no sudden arrival of any screws, there would then be another con stood outside a cell, where, inside, there would be half a dozen guys playing cards, for whatever currency. On this particular day, two blokes came down from another landing, in search of a big black guy called Samson, who was sat in on the card game. They broke a broom handle in half and made their way down to the 'game' cell, there was a hell of a set to and the next thing, they came running down the landing, both half battered, with big Samson stood outside the cell with both pieces of handle in his possession giving them a right ear bending, nothing different to any other day really, amusing though.

I only really had a couple of incidents while I was in there, the majority of cons in there were in for non violent crime but you're always going to come across some dick head who fancies giving you a smartening up. I was in the TV room one Saturday evening watching the football results and the guy next to me said he wanted 'twos up' on my smoke, which in nick terms means that you give him half your cig. Well, I thought, "fuck you mate" and smoked the damn thing, to which he took offence and threatened to kick my arse in the recess.

The whole room turned to view my reaction, so I said "fine, let's go and do it". Half way down the landing, this gob shite was saying that if I gave him a smoke, we could let it lie, his arse was well going and I collared him and told the twat that I was going to watch the TV and if he came anywhere near the room, I would open the fucker's head. Job done, without throwing a punch, all heads turned, I sat back in the same seat, lit up another smoke and no other fucker said a word, or asked me for 'two's' again……sorted. The second incident was on the football field, as I mentioned previously, I was one of those guys that could always score goals and there were always people that seemed to get pissed right off with that. An half cast Scouse kid with a really big gob played on the opposing side to me in quite a few games and was always mouthing off that the skinhead wanker up front would score if he wasn't marked. Well, I wasn't too bothered about the slur but it was when he started bawling it directly at me, then the time came for us to have words, I told that sack of shit that if he fancied a piece of me, then he'd better take his best shot. Bit of pushing and shoving and a few folk intervening to break up the squabble and that was that, he was larging it that he'd be visiting my landing to smarten me up, to which I replied that I'd be waiting and yet again, fuck all developed and the next time we crossed paths on the field, he seemed to lose his voice.

Christmas was a naff time to be caged up, a couple of days before the big day, there was a ginger geezer from Doncaster on our wing and he was adamant that he was going to spend Santa's night in his own bed. There'd be a good foot of snow on the ground at the time and the idiot had waited until the landings were locked and there all the cons were supposedly in their own cells, the next 'screw' check being at midnight. All cons still had access to the landings and the recess rooms but were trusted to 'behave' themselves with minimum supervision. Around 10.30, our would be escapee smashed one of the ground floor landing windows and jumped out into the snow, a blanket 'rope' with a mop bucket handle formed into a hook wrapped around himself. Off he went, through the snow and up towards the large plastic covered greenhouses, leaving a trail that a six year old could follow. We lost sight of him for a while and then we could see the snow falling from the forty foot fencing as the clown tried in vain to get the make shift hook on the end of his blanket rope to catch round the fence top. This went on for a while before the fence became still and we wondered whether or not the idiot had given up the ghost. A few minutes later, half a dozen burley screws trudged through the snow and passed the window from which we were viewing the entertainment, two of them were dragging the disgruntled ginger 'Houdini', who appeared to be wet through and half battered. So much for his attempt to reach Doncaster for Christmas, he only managed to get as far as the 'block' and solitary confinement!

We were all woken on Christmas Day morning by the sound of carols booming out of the tannoy system, which down very well, I can assure you. One or two cons took major exception to this and smashed the tannoys from their mountings with sweeping brushes, fair play but the back lash of that was that we were subjected to polishing the fucking landing for the rest of the morning! The tea urns came round to each landing and because of the occasion, we had the choice of tea or coffee, tremendous generosity from the powers that be. The Christmas dinner was quite bland but it did have all the requirements and we were all given an orange each, no crackers or hats but one can't expect everything! The day came and passed and I, for one, was happy to get it out of the way and crack on with the rest of my bird.

The festive season was riddled with power cuts due to the bad weather, which caused some major problems as the screws had to be on top of their game. One evening in the dining hall, the power dropped and in the darkness, a couple of screws got battered before the lights came back on, a bit difficult to point out any of the cons involved when no-one could see them!

I kept up with the football, rugby and visits to the gym in order to keep myself in reasonable shape, I always ate quite well too, I made sure that I had plenty of, Riveta crackers, honey and peanut butter to snack on out of meal times. The meals in nick were ok really, nothing brilliant but enough to keep you going, every Saturday and Sunday tea times, the order of the day was salad, which was ok I suppose but I was never a lover of beetroot and a portion of the diced up stuff was always served up. I only ate it because it was there but even to this day I tend to bypass that fucking horrible stuff!

It was around that time when the government were contemplating changing the remission laws, so everybody was constantly up to date with the news.

Easter soon came round and there was a couple of days 'holiday' for all us cons, there were competitions of all kinds arranged and a rugby match against the screws. It was a case of turning your mind off regarding the outside world and getting involved in the activities to pass more time. The rugby game kicked off and was going quite well until one of the cons got levelled by two screws and had to be carted off on a stretcher. The lad was a decent player and the two big bullying bastards purposely hit him from both sides and broke his ribs, well, the game turned into a bit of a 'mean machine' confrontation after that, quality entertainment.

I'd been making a caravan from matches for three months and I'd really gone to town on the detail, getting a few books from the prison library so that I could make it as realistic as possible. Everything worked on the thing, the doors all opened, the hay rack ob the back was active with little chains, the wheels all turned, the roof slid off and everything inside was detachable. A hell of a lot of lads in there made similar things to pass the time, so I made sure that this model was a cut above the rest and even fit a full breaking system to the under carriage. I made a couple of lanterns and fixed them on either side of the doors on the front, to make them more authentic, I took the eyelets out of my plimsolls, filled them with glue to give them the appearance of glass and attached them to the lantern body. All the sides and the roof were decorated in fancy carved matches and then the finished item was varnished and ready to send out into civi street. Cons from all over the nick would come down to get an eye full of my 'masterpiece' and a big drug barren came with his sidekick and offered me £125 for the for it, as he wanted to send it to his wife. We were only earning around three quid a week in there, so that was a massive amount of dosh and the guy said he would put the money into a bank account or bring me it down and pay me direct. He was quite aggrieved when I turned down his offer and I knew then that I had to get the thing out on my next visit, before it got destroyed or robbed, so within a few days, it was on its way to Bradford, safe and sound.

There's always some prat that will take a dislike to you, so keeping a reasonably low profile is in your best interest, let the gobshites attract all the attention and try not to lose any remission time. I recall watching a bit of TV one evening when a new arrival came and sat in the room; biggish lad just sat there and watched the box. A few minutes later, three guys came in and just laced the shit out of him, leaving him in quite a bad way. I walked out of the room before the alarm was raised, thinking he'd obviously upset somebody and didn't fancy facing a rake of questions from the screws. Apparently, he'd come from the Strangeways nick in Manchester and when he was in there he'd been a bit of a drug barren. Another con that had been transferred from Strangeways to Wymott a month earlier, had owed the barren quite a lot of dosh and skipped without paying. When he found out that the barren had arrived, he quickly put it about that the guy was a nonce and tried to turn the tables, so the big guy got a proper hiding due to the other lying toe rag trying to avoid one himself.....prison life. "Do not believe all you hear and do not tell all you see".

June 22nd arrived and I was out of there, my Uncle Pete came across to pick me up at the gates and in the motor with him, was Sue, great stuff. Back at my mum's house and my scooter was in the garage, taxed, insured and ready to drive away, Russ and the guys had it all sorted, quality. The lads had arranged a big party down at the Salthorn boozer, which was a belting do and was packed to the rafters, the shackles were off and I could start living again.

Chapter 8

Renolds, where I worked and was doing my apprenticeship, had kept my job open, mainly thanks to a Training manager called Dave Woolner, major thanks to him. I only had to do a couple of modules to complete the full apprenticeship, so that was finished in a breath and I was classed as a fully skilled engineer with a reasonable income, things couldn't be any better, or so I thought.

July 28th and work was shutting down for a full two weeks, everyone was off to ale houses in the area for a holiday piss up celebration. There were plenty of guys out and I was stupidly on the two wheels with my mate Simmo on the back. We'd done quite a few boozers and a lot of the lads made there way over to the Salthorn, most in taxis, with Simmo and myself following on the scoot. Beers were flowing well in there and one or two of the guys were trying to advise me to leave the wheels there and get a cab home but foolishly, I thought I knew better, so when the pub shut at 3pm, both Simmo and me put the helmets on and were on our way. About a mile up the road, there was a bend and the road cambers away from you, well, I'm not really sure what we did but Sim fell off and I slid across the road and hit one of those cast iron telegraph posts. I ended up on the grass verging and remember standing up, only to fall straight back down, staring up into the clear blue sky. The next thing

I recall is being strapped into a bed in the ambulance, with Simmo telling me to stop struggling and to keep still. In and out of consciousness and then into casualty at the Bradford Royal Infirmary, I was obviously in a major amount of shock and was shouting at the top of my voice for them to give me my jeans back so that I could be away on my toes…..some chance of that.

The law turned up and were obviously only interested in whether I was over the limit, not paying much attention as to the extent of my injuries. The doctors explained that it was possible that I could lose a limb and that there was no way that they could interview me in any shape or form. My mom and brother Bryan had arrived and were telling me that I was in a bad way and was facing amputation. With that, they gave me a general anaesthetic to stop me carrying on and the next thing I was up on the wards with both legs all strapped up with some doctor trying to explain the seriousness of my situation, I again drifted from consciousness.

Apparently, they pulled this top consultant called Mr Holmes in, to see if he could take over and smarten me up, he put me straight into theatre and got to work. I woke up the next day feeling like shit, with large casts on both legs, massive grazing down both arms and one hip, grazes down one side of the face and sporting a top black eye. Sue came in to see me and tried to put me in the picture, explaining that I was going to be in there for quite a while, great, I thought, out of one institute and straight into another! Mr Holmes came to see me and explained what the surgery consisted of; I'd seriously dislocated knees, taking the caps off and breaking them both. I'd severed the artery, almost all the ligaments and quite a lot of the nerves in the left leg and most of the ligaments and some of the nerves in the right leg. Bit of a mess really, Holmes had pinched a vein from my right wrist and managed to attach it, in line on the severed artery, the down side being that the circulation would always be at a slow flow. The left leg had gone black form the knee down and he told me that we had a five day period in which to see whether the surgery was a success or not, if it was the latter, then the limb would have to be amputated. When you're in that sort of situation, you realise just how precious your heath is and all the money in the world can't purchase that for you. On the fifth day, I woke up and pulled the covers back to see if there was any change in my predicament and to my relief, there were a few small pink dots on my toes, I just laid back and breathed a large sigh. The pressure of having my leg cut off was put to bed for the time being but later that day I insisted on seeing the house doctor because I couldn't seem to move my thumb on my left hand. He was well put out and told me that they'd x-rayed me from head to toe when I came in and that there was no way that there was a problem with the thumb. After a bit of a heated argument, he eventually agreed to have a portable x-ray machine brought in to scan the left hand thumb. The matron on the ward was a clever conceited bitch, who had no time for me and said that I deserved all I'd got because, in her opinion, the accident was drink related, she said that it was people like me that ruined other people's lives. It turned out that she was the talk of the ward, with all the nurses saying that she was having an affair with some married copper, so who was ruining other folk's lives there then? "Don't throw the stones from behind the glass!". Miss clever arse and myself had a few 'kick offs', I wasn't having this hypercritical cow dictating to me; hell it was tax payers dosh that was paying her bloody wages.

The meals in there were a lot worse than in the nick, so Sue would bring me food in every night at visiting time, it was a lot of pressure on the poor girl's shoulders but give her due praise, she was a brick throughout. All the guys would come visiting, most of them bringing me smokes and beers, so on a night, I'd lose myself inside a pair of head phones and a few ales. Long haul or not, I wasn't able to have any part of the running of the scooter club, so Russ took the reigns on that side. Even though I was laid there with both legs and one hand in plaster, I thought that I'd eventually mend and be back to my best. I pulled a doctor and demanded to know the total extent of my injuries, to which he told me in no uncertain terms, that I would never kick a football, run or walk without the aid of sticks ever again. I was absolutely wiped out, my whole world just fell to the ground, and I was shattered at the thought of being totally crippled for the rest of my life.

Things just didn't get any better, a couple more operations and then one afternoon, a young nurse came to remove some stitches from the back of my left knee but stopped after the cast and dressings were taken off. Doctors and nurses were there in droves, due to the inadequate monitoring of the staff, the wound had all infected, which resulted in me losing half the muscle just below the knee. They removed part of the muscle and then had to graft some skin, which was taken from the top of my thigh, onto the calf and back of the knee. Due to the severe nerve damage in the left leg, I had these massive bouts of pain, in which I would perspire so much that they had to change the bed cloths at least twice a day. So understanding, or just inexperienced, were the hospital staff, that they didn't believe me when I told them about the amount of pain I was in and when I explained to them that I had excruciating pain in my left heel, they just said that it was a slight movement of the nerves. Eventually, the guy from the plaster room came onto the ward and cut out the heel of the cast, low and behold, to the total embarrassment of the nurses, there was found to be a one inch spike of plaster that was embedded in my heel! Once that little incident was out of the way, they kept changing my casts for different types and I was eventually fitted up with a cast with hinges on either side of the knee. I was on a rehabilitation schedule with the phsyio department, which was damn hard graft and no easy ride, especially with three casts on my limbs. I thought I could 'escape' a couple of times but must have misunderstood the physio's slightly because when Chaz came to pick me up, he was shown the door that quick that I didn't even get to speak to him.

After being on a slow mend for four months, I was up and about taking a few steps at a time but the physio's told me that I wouldn't be allowed to leave until I could manage to get myself up and down two sets of stairs. With that carrot dangling in front of me I knew that I would only be a couple of days before I was on my way home. Two days later, I was sat in a wheel chair at the top of the steps with the thought that if I could manage this feat, then I'd be on my way out of the door and on the mend at home. The thumb on my left hand wasn't fixing too well and the ball joint at the base kept popping out each time they removed the cast, apparently the ligament had detached itself from the bone. So, with a cast on each leg and the left hand all potted up, I set about the staircase in the hospital, sweat was pouring out of me, I was absolutely soaked and the pain went straight through me. I stopped at the bottom of the stairs and composed myself, setting myself for the task of reaching the top and my goal of getting out of there. Each step I climbed was covered with the sweat that was dripping from my body, the pain had totally sapped all my strength, I was on auto pilot but determined to reach the top step. I grabbed the rail and with one last push, pulled my smashed up frame that final step, spun and collapsed into the wheel chair. I lay there smiling to myself, only to hear the physic say that we would try the task again the next day with some different 'rockers' on the feet of the casts. The shit hit the fan; I went ballistic and told her that I was on my way out of there that very same day, no matter what, reminding her of what she'd said regarding the climbing of the stairs. Nurses, doctors and physio's were all arguing the toss around me as I made my phone call to my mate Chaz, there was absolutely no way that I was staying in there another day. Within two hours, Chaz was wheeling me out of the ward and down towards the foyer, there were three or four nurses watching from the door as he slid me into the back of his Escort van……adios!!!

Sue and I were living in a flat above the hairdressers at Shelf and I managed the staircase on my backside, which was a damn site easier than hopping up and down on those bloody crutches. It was still a struggle getting about, most people on crutches have a good leg to hop on but both my legs were in cast, so weight on either one sent shooting pains through body and the cast on the hand didn't make it any easier! The doctors decided that the thumb would never mend properly and took the cast off, leaving me with the option of putting up with it or having it pinned, which would have probably left me with limited movement. I thought 'what the hell, I'll put up with it'.

When the casts came off for the last time, I had 'drop foot' on both legs due to all the ligaments being so badly damaged, I was devastated. "Reach for the Sky" comes to mind .....Douglas Barder, although I still had the pins, I didn't have a leg to stand on! The doctors said that I'd have to wear large callipers to assist me walking and that would probably never change. I was working round the clock, building the muscles up in my legs and I had decided to wear strong, sturdy boots to assist the ankles and feet, there was no way I was wearing those big calliper things. I was determined to get myself back to work and earning a crust, Sue and I had decided to get married, so I desperately needed to get back on an even keel with life.

The work thing was going well, I was working in the stores, on a light duty basis for a while, and then, when I was a lot stronger, I was back on the engineering side. Back home, I built a scooter from a lot of spares that we had between us and was soon back on the road, which went down like a lead weight with both Sue and my mom. I paid a visit to hospital and dropped off the walking sticks, callipers and crutches, Holmes, who had 'rebuilt' me, was absolutely astounded and when he realised that I'd arrived on two wheels, he almost fell off his chair. He couldn't believe how independent I'd become in such a short space of time but told me that in later life, my injuries would come back to haunt me.

Sue and I got married in Shelf in April 1983, the day went well, the weather was fine and the reception was top draw at a nice hotel/restaurant in Bradford called the Dubrovnik. Chaz played his part as Best Man and we even had bagpipes played outside the church by a big guy, who'd been in the scooter club years ago, called the gravedigger. He'd got the name from when he'd dug graves in Bingley, years previously, supposedly alongside Peter Sutcliffe, who became the Yorkshire Ripper…… small world! My granddad, on my dad's side unfortunately missed the wedding, as he'd passed on a couple of months before. He was a lovely man, always smartly dressed and always wore a hat, either a Trilby or Fedora type hat. He'd served in Tripoli in World War 2, although that was a subject that he would never talk about, he'd been in the textile industry most his life and there was always a photograph of him and Prince Charles on the sideboard, from when the pair had met in the seventies. Right out of the blue, he'd said to my Nan that he needed to go across and see my mom and the kids and with that, he made the two bus journey over to Toller Lane. We were all at my moms when he arrived, we were a bit perplexed as to why he'd suddenly turned up on his own for no real reason other than just to see that everyone was ok. He didn't stay too long and didn't have that much to say and then he was gone. He had a stroke that night, which he never came round from and the next day he passed away, it appeared that he'd made the journey to visit us, knowing that his time was up, a really nice chap and a massive loss to the family.

We went down to London for some quality honeymoon time and stayed at the Rembrandt hotel in Knightsbridge, London, a really nice few days. I'd been to London when I was younger with school and quite a few times whilst following the mighty Leeds but this time was different. Sue and I went all over the capital, viewing as many sights as we could possibly fit in during our stay.

In June 1884, Sue gave birth to a lovely daughter who we named Lucy. I was there at the birth and it was the most joyous feeling I have ever experienced, a little person born into the world that was a part of me. We arrived home with our little bundle of joy; the nursery was all ready in a house that we'd bought and was in the process of decorating throughout. Around that time, Russ married Sue's sister Margaret, Chaz married Alison and Bri married Mandy, the girl he'd met at Bradbury Hall. I was best man for both Chaz and Brian; the 'Zip' did the honours for Russ. We had a coach trip to Manchester before Brian got hitched, which was a decent night on which plenty of 'lush' was downed. We did fuck up slightly when we all entered a boozer that turned out to be full of Man City fans but it didn't really stir until we were leaving. A bit of verbal kicked in and them a couple of Mancs got 'bashed' before the whole ale house went up and there were glasses bodies and chairs flying everywhere. We had the upper hand and the City boys never came outside to carry on what had started inside......... lawmen on the scene and we were away. It was on that trip that I first met a guy called Brian Pollard, long blonde hair and a big Leeds fan.

I was still making one in with scooter club and going on the odd 'run', we did the Hawes trip, with a few of the old crew still in tow. We were having a few jars in the Green Dragon on the lunchtime session and having a good old laugh before going to the large fete in the village. We were fooling about outside the pub and things got a little bit heated and before I realised what had happened, 'stop starting' Martin had stabbed me in the fucking knee with a large camping knife! It was a blade similar to the 'piece' in the film, Crocodile Dundee!! Chaz, who had taken the number one position, butted him in and gave him it, while I got strapped up in the boozer. He was called 'stop starting' because he only worked now and again, when he felt like it. We managed to see a doctor in the village and he sorted me out with a rake of stitches, which hurt like hell without any anaesthetic, he then turned me over and fired too big injections into my arse, one penicillin and one tetanus. The doc said that I had to refrain from the intake of alcohol fro 24 hours, yeh right. Down to the fete and on the cider in the beer tent, fighting with the pillows on the long log and generally getting involved in anything we could. The trip home was difficult, trying to ride the scoter and keep the leg as straight as possible.

Every thing we had was going into the house and the baby, Sue was working all hours around the child, hairdressing and I had just changed jobs and gone to work in air conditioning. Times were hard but we were happy and making ends meet, I was working a hell of a lot of hours in the air conditioning game, which I quite enjoyed but Sue had passed her driving test and we wanted a car, which meant we needed some more income. I was still riding on two wheels, I'd had, in total, 1 Lambretta, 12 Vespa's and two Yamaha's, one being a big 750 D.O.C but seriously needed to change to four wheels. There weren't many options open for more income, I was a decent engineer and by now but overtime wasn't always guaranteed and there wasn't any call for 'moonlighting' engineers! I was always quite handy, was in half reasonable condition, so I thought I could hold my own in confrontations but working the doors wasn't really what I'd got in mind but sometimes we just have to do what needs to be done. "Don't wait for your ship to come in, brave the cold and swim out to it!".

Chapter 9

Dean, a lad who played pool in the same pub league as I did, worked at a place called Beau Brummell's over in Guisley and he'd heard that I was looking for a start on the doors. We discussed the details and I agreed to start the job the following week, I got kitted out in black and whites, a nice new pair of lace up dealer boots and was ready to face the music. There were four guys on the door shift, two on the door and two on the large dance floor area of the club. The entrance was quite tight with a small foyer and a desk with a till on it, Andy, the gaffer or one of the girls, would sit and the desk and collect the dosh. Underneath the small desk, were a couple of rounder's bats, to assist us if situations got out of hand. There was a rota for the nights to be worked and after a couple of weeks; I was on every Friday and Saturday night. The place was always packed, plenty of women in and there were always lots of groups of guys, the only drawback was that the groups came from all the different surrounding areas, so there was always somebody kicking off. Our working crew was, myself, Dean, Paul Rigby and either J.P, Oz or a guy called Pete. Pete was sound but after a while he seemed to lose all interest after coming off second best in a bit of a set to one weekend, so that was him, out of the game.

Two other guys that I worked with in the air conditioning had stated to work doors also, Trev

Cruxon and Paul Airey. They were both working in Bradford at different manors but Trevor said he needed a change so we brought him on board with us over at Brummell's. Trev was a sound guy, a biggish, thick set lad who had a head like one of those concrete balls that they use on Worlds Strongest Man and whoever he butted went down like a sack of shite. He'd only been working with us for a couple of nights when we had a quality kick off, the place was heaving, I was upstairs, with Trev facing me from the other side of the dance floor. J.P had come up to the bar and got involved with five or six blokes who were well up for it, I saw him arguing with them and it looked to be getting a bit heated. I pushed through the crowd of punters just as the punches started flying, as soon as we had hold of a couple of them, it seemed to calm down, until J.P let go of his lad and the fucker spun round and landed one right in my 'dish'. The shit hit the fan and anyone in striking distance copped for it, the lads in question got it and right, there was a kid dressed all in white and he came running through everyone, straight at me but I stepped right onto him and took him out in one. Within minutes, the music is always put back on and the punters are all dancing as if nothing has happened. It's always better to try and move these incidents into the doorway but unfortunately, it doesn't always go to plan.

Brummell's was a decent gaff and I enjoyed being there, the bar staff were sound, the guys in our crew were sound and Andy, who owned the place, was also sound. He was only 22 at the time, a tall guy who thought he could do a bit and take care of himself, which wasn't really true, he got knocked over a few times and I can't recall him ever coming out on top, nevertheless, he was ok. This was a time before the door licensing laws had come to the fore, so we would always have a few beers while working, nothing major, always half pint glasses and more often than not, we would end up having some feed before going home.

The scooter club was still going strong and were meeting at Junction pub over near the top of White Abbey, Bradford and I was still making one in with the likes of Bri, Russ and of course Chaz. One Meeting night we went down town to the Flagship boozer where quite a few small groups of scooter lads used to met up, including some Gemini members from Leeds. Joe 90 had been taking some verbal from a guy called Ravi and was looking to sort it out. Both were Kung Fu whiz kids and were on British Squads, so it was going to be interesting. The pub was as busy as fuck and there were around eighty guys who were obviously backing Ravi. We were around 12 strong but were outnumbered 7/8 to one as the pub emptied onto the street. Joe and Ravi were punching and kicking shite out of each other with that Kung Fu stuff for a good fifteen minutes before Joe caught Rav under the chin and knocked him out. His head hit the floor with a load crack and claret spilled all over the pavement. I heard one kid saying that there were only a dozen of us and they should smarten us all up while they had the chance. We made our way to the Pack Horse pub at the top of the town, making sure to walk at a slow pace and not to run. I remember Chaz saying that if the mob made a move towards us, to gat weighed in and start swinging our crash helmets for all we were worth. The mob didn't pursue us and even though were waited a half hour in the pub, we didn't get any grief.

I wasn't really doing much with the footie at the time but did manage to get to the odd game. Leeds got to the FACup semis, which was held at Hillsborough, Sheffield against Coventry. I went with Chaz and although we didn't get involved in any rumbles, there were bits and bats going off for the majority of the day. We were in the Leppings Lane end of the ground and it was absolutely manic!! We were all crammed in by the law and the amount of bodies far exceeded the capacity allowance. You had no control over where you were supposed to be stood and I remember thinking that if anyone fell over, they would be trampled to death. Young fans were crying and the fear was etched on plenty of scared faces. Some fans were climbing up, or being lifted up to the top tier of the stand to try and avoid being crushed. We lost the game in extra time 3-2 and we were devastated. Two years later in the exact same end, same circumstances ....the Liverpool fans were not so lucky. The problems that were encountered by the Leeds fans in '87 are rarely mentioned but if the stewards and the Law had bothered to take them on board, then the deaths of all those Liverpool fans might have been avoided.

My Granddad, on my mum's side, died at that time, he'd moved over to Lancaster about ten years previously and was living with Betty, his second wife. He was on an oxygen bottle most of the time but the tough old guy would still occasionally get in his motor and drive all the way over to see the family. He could be a real grumpy and short tempered bloke at times but I could sit down and have some great chats with him, he was a really knowledgeable man and could hold a decent conversation on anything from boxing to politics. He knew he was near deaths door and had been battling with the councils to get relocated in Bradford, so that Betty would be near family. We got him moved back over to Bradford in April 1987, we managed to get him settled and I sat chatting with him about the Sugar Ray Leonard v Marvin Haglar fight that was taking place that night. I think his last push in life was to get Betty back near the family and that was his goal, he died in his sleep that very night, God bless him.

We moved house and once again money was tight, so I was working three nights a week for a while on the door at Brummells, as well as working as many hours as I could in the day job. Rigby had got a 6 month stretch for breaking some guy's jaw, so he was off the rota, unfortunate really, he was a body builder and not only did he look the part, he was a damn good doorman. As I recall, the bloke in question had been ejected from the premises and had tried to take a cheap shot from behind Rigby had defended himself and the guy hit the deck but the self defence aspect was thrown out by the 'beak' and Rigby was in the 'big house'.

The local football team at Yeadon, just up the road from Guisley, had won the cup and they were all in celebrating, they were filling the cup from the top shelf and were definitely in high spirits. The main kid kept dropping his trollies and even though I'd warned him a couple of times, I knew we were in for a ruck. Once again his pants came down and the bird was out of the cage, so to speak. The guy definitely didn't want to leave and as I pulled him from the dance floor, his mates intervened and a bit of a scuffle took place but we managed to get three or four of them down the steps and through the main door. The kid with the trousers was going barmy and shouting that he wanted a piece of Dean and that he thought we were all wankers. The big guy at his side was supposedly a very handy bloke and was always there as the trouser kids muscle. They were kicking the door in and Dean flew straight out, dropping the kid with a good slap, the muscle tried a cheap shot but stopped in mid track when I moved forward, he spun round but I caught him with an uppercut, putting him on his arse, next to his mate. All his mouth and nose were covered in claret and he just looked up at me, trying to comprehend what had just happened, I didn't have to follow it up, there was only one winner. Job done, the two main guys sat on their buts and nothing coming back from the rest of their lads.

Things were going well at work and we were doing ok at Brummell's but one should never get complacent in any walk of life and one night I was caught off guard in the club one night. A tall guy was slumped on the bar and as I went over to ask him to straighten him up and ask him if he was ok, he suddenly came to life and lifted me clean off the floor. My arms were stuck by my sides and I was in such a position, that I couldn't break free, butt him or kick him. The guy spun with his arms locked firmly around me, I was literally head and shoulders above everyone in the club, he then threw me straight onto the nearest table. It was a long table, with about ten drinks on it and I landed right in the middle, smashing all the bloody glasses, as I looked up, the bastard's fist came crashing into the middle of my 'dial', smashing my nose and putting me out of the game for a second or two. I quickly rolled off the table to cover up as he stuck the 'Timpson' in, this was a bad situation for any doorman to be in and I managed to grab hold of his legs and bring him down to floor level. There was a bit of a struggle before I could scramble to my feet but once up, I landed a couple of big hitters into his jaw. He didn't even flinch and was trying to get up, eyes glazed and screaming at the top of his voice, it was then that I put a full bodied right hander straight into his throat, a dangerous shot but I didn't have any choice. The incident had only taken a couple of minutes and back up had then arrived but if the pillock had been quick enough to do me with a glass while I was on the table, I would have been well smartened.

We were at it almost every night at that gaff, not that it was a really rough hole; it was just that there were lads from all the different areas. I regularly went home with a jacket sleeve torn off or half a shirt on and occasionally via the hospital for a couple of stitches, no big deal really. I once had to go for a couple of stitches and a couple of jabs in the arse after some prat bit a hole in my side. Two brothers had kicked off and I ended up freefalling down the full flight of steps with one of them firmly attached to my side with his teeth....very nice. He was like a pit bull terrier and just would not let go, until one of the lads had closed off his windpipe, the law came and said that the two brothers had been taken to hospital and tried to charge a couple of us with assault but dropped the investigation when they'd got the facts.

Andy, the lad in charge, said that he was going to move over to Pateley Bridge near the Dales and get a boozer out there. Both me and Dean new what Brummell's could take and thought it would be a top move for us to get in there, with the help of one of the brewery's. We could both muster up our part of the cash, through family connections and the brewery would stump up the rest. We had meetings on top of meetings but the guy we were dealing with from Mansfield Brewery was pissing all over our shoes and in the end it all fell apart.

It was at that time, that I was drinking in the Fairweather Green pub, a pub where my uncle Pete frequented along with quite a few other lorry drivers. It had emerged that Sutcliffe, the Ripper, used to go in there from time to time but it was said that he generally just had a couple of beers and kept to himself. I became a bit of a regular and it was from there we went on Wembley weekends for the rugby league cup finals. These were great weekends away, setting off on the Friday morning and returning late on Sunday. For the first couple of years, we had tickets for the ABA boxing finals at Wembley Arena as well as tickets for the rugby league cup final on the Saturday. We saw the likes of Nigel Benn and one or two other up and coming decent boxers of the time. I recall on one of the trips, whilst most of our party was checking into our hotel in Earls Court, an Arab gent came running into the foyer shouting and generally playing fuck. After calming the situation down, it came apparent to the staff that one of our lads had pissed out of the window into his open topped motor, which was parked on the street!!! It took quite a lot of apologising and negotiation to stop us all being thrown out. It was a great deal, as the trip was really well run and organised very well. I went on the rugby weekend trips for a few years from the Fairweather and played darts for them for quite a while. At the time, the Fairweather was a decent boozer and winning the yearly darts knockout was nothing to be scorned at, so when I lifted the trophy for the one and only time, I managed a little smile....to say the least. I then went on to win the local Morgan's

Rum trophy for the chance to go and play in the preliminaries for the News of the World title. The event was held in Stockport and Russ came with me, as we thought we'd make a decent weekend of it. I was flattened in the first round of the tournament and we headed for Fallowfield, Manchester, where my brother Pete was based, while he was at university doing Law. Hence to say, we had a damn good drink and a laugh about the darts!

There was a guy who went on a couple of the trips from the Fairweather pub with us called Phil Robinson, a local bloke who was a joiner and had started doing some door work for a bit of extra cash. He was a tall bloke who got on well with most people and not really the 'doorman' type really. He always tried to compare places of work with me and was always adamant that his 'gaff', the 42nd Street, was the more difficult place to work at. I used to laugh and joke with him over this opinion and never really thought of Phil as a big handy lad, he was just an ok bloke that had the bottle to do the job. He had some kind of confrontation on the door one night and was followed after he'd finished work. The result was that Phil was killed, after being attacked and fatally injured by three men who had ambushed him and assaulted him with weapons. A terrible waste of life, Phil was never a violent guy, just a normal bloke making a few extra quid.

Back in the air conditioning game, the main man, Steve Lawther had sold out to a larger concern and conditions rapidly changed in the working arrangements. Steve had bought a large building near the University on the outskirts of Bradford town centre and was quickly having it revamped from top to bottom, in order to open it as an up market club. Trevor, Paul Airey, myself and one or two other guys went to work on the door of this new gaff, which was opened as the Rio Campus. It was a really plush manor and we were kitted out in white tuxedo jackets and black trousers. I wasn't too keen on the jackets and told Steve that as soon as we had any grief on the door, the jackets would be shagged. His reply was that, the sort of clientele that would be frequenting the place would be well above that, I just laughed to myself and realised that this side of life was a bit alien to him. It was all shirts and ties to start with, no exceptions but with that, all the half wrong kids just came, all dressed up in their best kit. After two weeks, I saw a lad on the dance floor, who was dressed in a black suit, throw a punch at a guy and before he'd hit the floor, the lad had kick him straight in the side of the head......out cold. I was on the lad in a breath and managed to get him into the foyer, what he wasn't going to do was nobody's business. We had a good old set to and I belted him all the way down the steps but he just turned tail and came straight back at me. The bloke was covered in claret but just wouldn't stop, two or three times I knocked ten bells out of him and it wasn't until he was at the bottom of the steps for a third time, that he threw the towel in, he just lit a smoke up and walked off, saying that he'd see me soon! It's situations like that, when you start to think that you could possibly end up with a death on your hands. Anyway, the white jacket was stained in the 'red stuff' and shortly after, we were all in the traditional black and whites, which brought Steve back down to earth and his dream of highly exclusive club was slowly disappearing. The lad who I'd had the set too with was apparently a Clayton guy called Andy, who had a twin, which was amusing over the next few weeks, while I tried to get to grips with which one was barred!

Trevor and myself decided we could make some decent 'wedge' doing a bit of debt collecting, so we set up a little business and had some cards printed. We worked on 30% commission but did all the leg work, no matter how far and charged nothing unless we got a result. We had some nice touches, we were picking clients up from all over the place and business was half decent. The odd contract occasionally cost us though, one Sunday morning, we were on our way over to the Moss Side estate in Manchester, it was pissing it down and I had a puncture on the bloody motorway, tremendous. I got it sorted and pulled off at the next services to fill up and as I did so, I was watching the pump position and just touched the car in front of me on the forecourt. It was hardly a touch really but I apologised to guy who's vehicle it was but he was adamant that I was a tosser and started on shouting and bawling. Trev just laughed and read the paper while I tried to calm the bloke down, he had his wife and kids in the car, so I couldn't understand why he was carrying on so much. I just carried on putting the juice in while he went to the kiosk but when he came back, he started on at me again and as he gave me a shove, I dropped the pump nozzle and gave him a straight right. He picked himself up and got in his car, quiet as a mouse but as he drove off, his kids were staring at me out of the back window, I felt shit but the geezer should have known his limitations, especially when he had the family with him. We arrived in Manchester and set about finding our destination, which turned out to be right smack bang in the middle of the massive estate. These places are pretty much no go areas but we were determined to find our 'mark' and discuss the debt. We pulled up outside the house; I got the paperwork ready and knocked on the house door. An Asian woman came to the door and when I explained who I was looking for; a bloke came forward and said that was he. I showed him the paperwork and the debt of £3000, to which he took a step backwards and said that it was his brother's debt and he didn't live there. This was my guy, no doubt about it but he just denied it, so while we're having a stand up verbal, Trev started blasting the car horn and on turning round, I saw that half the bloody street were coming out onto the road. They were all asking who I was, what I wanted and to get fucked off. This situation wasn't good and one or two of the pillocks were chucking things at the motor, as more and more of the residents poured onto the road. The Asian guy tried to push me from the step, so I quickly 'walled' him up and sat him on his shitter, telling him I'd be seeing him later. Down the steps and onto the road, people moved out of my way but were still giving me plenty of verbal but there far too many bodies to even contemplate having a ding dong. As we drove off at speed, there one or two boots into the back end of my BMW but we were in no doubt what the outcome would have been if we had stopped. A totally bad day at the office, flat tyre, petrol station confrontation, dents in my motor and not one penny recovered.

I'd changed the day job and gone back to Renolds, working four nights a week, which was fine for some door work and also fit in well for collecting a few debts. The downside was that Sue and I were drifting apart and it wasn't long before we called it a draw and decided that the best thing was for us to part ways. I was kept well busy and had three incomes ticking over. I started seeing a girl called Gloria, who'd been doing a bit of barmaid work and occasionally working the 'door till' in the Rio club. I was seeing my daughter Lucy two or three times a week and had bought a small house in Wyke on the outskirts of Bradford.

I went to get some sun for a week, in Tenerife with Dean. We got stopped at customs after arriving at the airport and rushed off to a room with four soldiers. They were all armed and ranting and raving in 'native' tongue, with our passports getting passed from one to another!!?? We were kept for half an hour and then released, without one word of explanation, in fact, not one word of English directed at us! We had a great week, the weather was hot, the place was buzzing and we chilled through the day and partied at night. There was just one blip really, we were in a bar one night, when the law came bursting in and started whacking the shite out of guy with their batons. He was taking a right beating in the middle of the boozer and offering no resistance, so both me and Dean tried to reason with the lawmen but one of them spun round and stuck his gun straight in my face, telling me to go away. Seeing the narrowing of his eyes…..I held up my hands and slowly backed off, I didn't need to be told twice!!

Gloria and I had hit it off like a house on fire and were like two teenagers in each others company, we had loads in common and spent quite a lot of time in each others company but it all came to a halt. I had to make a choice, a new life with this girl who I'd totally fallen for and could see a long future with, or dig deep and try to make my marriage work. For years after, I often wondered if

I'd made the right decision and knew that I'd left a piece of my heart with Gloria.

I went back to live with Sue and Lucy and when I look back now, it was probably for all the wrong reasons, I still loved Sue but my daughter was the most important person in my world and she needed me in her life. That Christmas, the three of us went and stayed at the Sheraton Hotel in Blackpool, it cost a bloody fortune, the most expensive four days of my life but the experience of being waited on hand and foot, 24 hours a day over the Christmas period is one I'll never forget. We chilled out totally and I think I put a bloody stone on in those few days!!

In '91' Dean and I went on the Wembley weekend from Furnace pub, which was organised by Trev Walsh, he was a good laugh and a bit of a wide boy! That was a cracking trip with some great lads........Battys, Kinder, Goodall, Timmy Southgate, Jowett, Algie and a rake of others. Jim, Tim and myself were dressed as Musketeers on the match day and held traffic up all over Covent Gardens with our 'One for all' antics! Dean was supposed to be the forth Musketeer but we 'lost' him! We stopped off in a small village on the way back and were all looking forward to a 'nice' drink, when the landlord kicked off, shouting and carrying on, saying that Jim and Timmy had caused a rake of damage the year before and we all had to fuck off !! It took quite a while to convince him that none of us had ever been near his boozer before and he eventually agreed to serve us all. I'm not so sure he totally believed us but the 'session; went down without a hitch thankfully. Unfortunately the trip ended on a bad note with a Bradford lad called Barry Chapman having a near fatal accident. It was a top of the range coach, one of those half tier downstairs and full tier upstairs jobs and we were heading back up the motorway, all singing, boozing, playing cards etc, when Barry leant on the large exit door. The door flew open and he suddenly disappeared through it, ending up, bouncing down the road surface at around 70 mph!!! He was badly for quite a while, having quite a lot of skin ripped off and covered in cuts bruises and abrasions. I'm not sure of the full extent of his injuries but as far as I'm aware, he fully recovered. Apparently I think it was proved that there was a fault with the exit door.

Photo texts:-

Vespa P200E

Posing for the magazine.

Mark Minton, Keith Gardner, myself & the infamous skull.

The great Duncan Edwards with my great mum.

Me, Bryan, Pete & Pam

Pam, me, Pete & Bryan

Door Licence…….an 'iffy' looking 007.

Three Musketeers. Jim, Timmy & Me

Lyke Wake Walk. Womer, Me & Chaz

The badge of the Elite.

BD8 & BEYOND

DAVID MOULDS

BD8 & BEYOND

DAVID MOULDS

BD8 & BEYOND

Chapter 10

Times were changing rapidly, a lot of law firms were introducing Debt recovery lines and working at around an 8% charge which soon pushed myself and Trevor out of the game.

The majority of doors in the big cities up and down the country were run by two or three firms, yet in the West Yorkshire area, especially in Bradford, there were quite a few different teams and one firm seemed to be interested in taking over the whole shooting match at the time. Dean and I decided to get in on the action and make ourselves some decent earnings. We were soon in the frame and were supplying a few manors with good, solid guys, who could do a decent job. Dean was down at Cleckheaton, where there were three clubs and he'd soon sorted the supply out for all three, I went down and met all the guys concerned, a really good team of lads. One of his lads down there was Gary Kinder and we became really good mates over the years, a true friend of mine who I still see a lot of and speak with regularly. We were adding doormen to our team steadily and we were putting in more time and effort as we grew. I'd changed day time jobs again and was working as a maintenance engineer at a place in Pudsey near Leeds, a straight 39 hour a week job, which left me enough time to concentrate on the doors.

Saturday afternoon's were filled up with family commitments most of the time but I still managed to get to a few home games at Elland Road. Leeds won the 1st division title in the 91/92 season, which then changed to the Premiership and was restructured.

The Door staff registration scheme was being introduced and a hell of a lot of decent door lads were getting rejected when applying for licenses. Decent bouncers were generally blokes that had done the rounds and then decided to earn some wedge for controlling the bother, very much in the mode of 'poachers turning to game keeping'. Myself and Trev went on the first registration course in Bradford in 1993; we had to do three 2 hour sessions, which were held on Wednesday evening. One session was related to the identification of drugs and how to deal with drug related incidents. The instructor who took that particular part of the training was a blast from the past for me, Brian Noble, whom I'd gone to school with in the sixties, he later went on to achieve great things in the game of rugby league. There was a bit of first aid involved, a bit of self defence and how to deal with the public in general, without getting into a physical confrontation. The majority of the course was common sense really and related to aspects of the job that most of us were already up to speed with. It came across to me that the main object of the course and registration was for the law's benefit, so they could keep tabs on everyone that was working the doors. The licences were only compulsory to any door staff that were working inside city centre boundary, so you could still get away with employing any Tom, Dick or Harry in pubs and clubs that were outside that area. It's always more reassuring when the guys you are working with are good pals 'cos you know that they're more likely to cover your back with more conviction. Trev, Bri Hudson, Joe'90',

Airey, Kev Hodge, Gary, Lee, Stevie, Abi, the list goes on, even Russ did a short stint but it wasn't his cup of tea.

My life schedule was once again getting clogged up, I was still in the 39 hour a week maintenance job, running and working doors and I'd decided to take a City & Guilds in Electrical installation to put with other qualifications in Mechanical engineering and Air Conditioning. It was a tough period but by working up to 20 hours on some days, I managed to pass the course and acquire the qualification.

There were quite a lot of raves going on then and clubs were becoming rife with drugs. I stressed to all our guys that this was a no go area and if they wanted a piece of that kind of action, then they'd best find themselves other manors to work in. Now, I've met and worked with hundreds of doormen, some great guys, some just good doormen and of course, some bullies and some complete arse holes. There's always someone ready to nick a piece of what you've got and it was the same with the doors, people trying to undercut you, poach your lads or just trying to make you look bad. We had a few altercations with other teams that were trying to poach our lads and they were sorted out in no uncertain terms. On the flip side to that, I went up to a club called The Sports bar at Thornbury, Bardford, which was run by an 'oldish' body building guy called Les. There was a lad working on the door for him called Richard, a bloke that you definitely wanted on your side and I offered him more wedge to come and work on one of our doors. He jumped at the chance and as we left the gaff, Les was calling me all the cunts under the sun and telling me never to set foot in the manor again, fine but my need for Richard the 'Bulldog' was greater than his.

For the big raves of the time, the organisers would hire the Rio club and bring all there own people, i.e., DJ's, sound people and bouncers. There would be around six of us working on the inside of the club and six 'outsiders' working on the door, with approximately 1200 punters. On one occasion there was a big black guy in, who was rumoured to be a main dealer, he was the centre of attention and was wearing one of those 'puffer' type jackets and a Trilby type hat. The gaff was packed and everyone was shoulder to shoulder, if it had kicked off, it would have been serious mayhem. I pulled the 'dealer' straight away and stressed to him that if I saw anything slightly out of order, he would be out on the concrete. He just laughed at me and said he had 30 'runners' inside who were all carrying blades and that I would be a dead man at the drop of his hat! He opened his coat to prove his point and there in all its glory was a large machete on the inside. I looked round and wasn't surprised to see that I was totally surrounded by a dozen guys whose eyes were all fixed on my good self. I stated that what I'd said still stood and I pushed my way through his mob of 'runners' and made my way to the door. I'd worked with some of the lads that were manning the door before and they'd been fine but although I knew the two body builders that were there, I'd never stood on a door with them. I told them that they'd fucked up and let those fuckers in, carrying drugs and blades but it seemed to fall on deaf ears, they just told me to chill out and calm down. These prats were just going through the motions and I told them that if any of our guys got cut, then they would be the ones copping for it later. Shortly after, we had a couple of those damn 'runners' slung out of one of the side doors but to my amazement, half an hour later, we spotted them back in the thick of it. We collared them and they just laughed, stating that the lads on the door had taken a back-hander and that there was no way we could control the event. The guys on the door were respected bouncers and well known throughout Bradford at the time. Among them were a couple of guys, whom I'd known for years and I was devastated to find out that we could have been seriously injured or worse because they had supposedly 'rolled' over for a few pieces of fucking silver! I can picture their faces to this day and could name and shame them but they'd no doubt deny it and try and sue my arse.

We'd recruited a lot of new guys, Blackbelt Brothers Bob and Ian Siree, Jim Goodall, Andy Long, Dave York, Barry, Steve, Jimmy Donnelly and quite a few other decent blokes. We would rota the chaps out to different manors and would, more often than not, try to keep the same staff on the same doors as much as possible, so they new the punters, the set ups and working format.

Every other week in the Rio, we seemed to have an altercation with some of the Lidget Green, Queensbury or the Clayton lads, it seemed there was a never ending flow of them. One Saturday night quite a big crew of Clayton guys had infiltrated in small groups and were involved in various incidents which included the odd slap and lifting the odd handbag. One of their main blokes, a geezer called Bradbury was fingered by a bird for lifting her bag, so I pulled him into the foyer to question him. The bag turned up elsewhere, empty and a couple of his mates told us they'd wreck the joint if we didn't leave Bradbury alone. We were 6 strong against 30 plus and the shit hit the fan and right, ten to fifteen minutes of solid scrapping is quite a lengthy time and it took that long before the 'Old Bill' turned up. The mob steamed outside, 'levelling' a young copper and a WPC in their wake. The ends of the road had been blocked with Transit vans but the only 'mush' arrested was Bradbury. Chair legs, glasses, cloakroom poles and God knows what else were involved. We were slightly the worse for wear, battered and bloodied but nobody went to casualty and we managed to work out our shift. I remember Jimmy Donnelly saying he was glad we didn't have a set too like that every night or we'd all be in the 'knackers' yard or the morgue, sooner rather than later!!! I've crossed paths with quite a few of the guys involved on that night since in different incidents, John Softly, Mick Robbo and one or two others, who ironically were with the Leeds Service Crew ....small world. Mick Robbo however, went on to become and still is, a good mate of mine. I heard that Bradbury died of a drug related incident years later.

There were plenty of handy guys from around the Clayton area, some knobheads but on the flip side....some decent guys. Glen Marriot played plenty of rugby and was well pally with Dean and Kinder. We always exchanged greetings when meeting and would 'chew the fat' in passing. A handy, stand up bloke and also a solid Man U fan who moved with the Bradford Reds and occasionally ran with the Salford Reds. To this day we reminisce over 'run-ins' with Leeds and the Reds. His brother Neil is also another decent stand up guy that could always hold his own.

I was playing darts for the School Green pub at the time, with my good friend Gordon Ashley and my uncle Pete. We had some great times in the Green, we'd sometimes play darts on a Sunday afternoon, it would be 'Coach & Horses' pairs, with the winners stopping on and Gordon and myself usually kicked arse and won quite a few beers. Gordon looked like Mike Harding, the singer; he was a great laugh and was always cracking jokes and singing. We had to keep an eye on him though, as he was a diabetic, he knew he wasn't doing his condition any good whatsoever but said that he would enjoy his life while it lasted and when the 'reaper' came, he would throw his hand in. He worked in the glass industry and would do the diamond leaded windows, he was top draw and put anything in a window, he even did quite a bit of work on the York Cathedral. If I wasn't at the footie or had any other commitments at that time, I would make one in at The Fleece pub in Allerton. Gordon and a few others did a 'tea time' club in there which was a good laugh. Another guy I knew that frequented the place was a boxer named Tony Penn. He was a quality puncher in his day and was offered a place down at the famous Terry Lawless gym in London on the proviso that he kept out of trouble and changed his social circle. Hence to say, he didn't and missed his big chance. I once let him and a couple of his mates into the Rio, which was a bad call on my part because when they were 'fronted' up by around ten blokes on the edge of the dance floor the 'boxers' had no problem with the opposition!

Sunday nights saw the introduction of 'house' and 'garage' music in the Rio, this was hard work because the lighting was turned down low and with all the punters being black, you couldn't see a thing in the alcoves and the corners. Now I've nothing against anyone smoking draw, weed, hash or anything else really but if I could help it, it wasn't going to happen in any manor that I was working in. There was a big guy in dungarees just down from the main bar and I could see that he was 'skinning' up, so I made my way over to him and explained that this wasn't going to happen inside the club. He jut carried on making his joint and asked what the fuck I was going to do about it, to which I replied, I would bin him straight out of the door. There was howls of laughter and he said "If you haven't noticed white man, you're surrounded by my brothers and I'll be going nowhere". I looked round, hoping for some back up but all I saw was a sea of black guys, all laughing. A tricky situation but I stuck with it, telling the big guy that if he lit the smoke, I'd definitely take him out, so it would be in his best interest to smoke it outside and then come back in. He said there was no way that he'd be allowed back in and that he was going to smoke it where he stood. I looked him straight in the eye and screamed at him to light the fucking thing or get some fresh air, "one or the other but do it now and stop fucking me about!". To my surprise he said he would smoke it outside as long as I came and told the lads on the door to let him back in, nice result and I turned and led him through his 'brothers' to the door. Quite a few of those punters followed suit as the night went on and at kick out time, the big guy came and shook my hand, thanking me for a good evening.

Battle of the Bands rounds were held at the Rio club and even the final for a couple of years running. On one occasion, the rounds had been held at the Rio but the final had been scheduled to be held at Bradford University. I got on well with a couple of the resident doormen from the Uni, one of whom was a guy called Johnna, a punk guy who ran with the Leeds Service

Crew. I'd always had time for Johnna, he was a bloke who had bottle and a guy with some half decent morals. Anyhow, it was arranged that me and my lads would be running the doors for the Battle of the Bands finals at the Uni. We had two on the front door and two inside from 12 noon 'till 6p.m and the same from 6p.m 'till midnight. Jim Goodall and Trev on the door and myself inside with John Pye were on for the 'early' shift, after that, we went to work elsewhere. The day was going fine, with the bands belting out their stuff and the fans drinking plenty. It was a sunny day and quite a lot of fans were allowed to move in and out, as long as they were stamped. One incident left a sour taste though, a 'loser' from Stoke was on the large dance floor drinking from a glass and I 'pulled' him and told him to leave the area or the drink. As I left the floor, there was some commotion behind me and apparently, the lad had attempted to jump me from behind and John had 'dropped' him. We threw the lad out of the side exit, only to see him run at the 12ft x 6ft window and launch a large rock at us. The glass went everywhere, showering quite a lot of people; luckily no-one was badly injured. I followed the lad up the grass embankment towards the road where all the coaches were parked and just as I made a grab for him, he jumped on a coach and spun round, hitting me straight over the head with a glass 'Pils' bottle that he pulled from the dashboard. I was stunned for a second or two and bleeding from the head wound but the lad had no real escape and as I caught him, we both dropped five feet to the road through the emergency exit at the rear of the bus. I gave the fucker a good bashing before dragging him back to the venue where the 'Old Bill' picked him up. About an hour later, the lad was back at the Uni and the law were trying to arrest me for assaulting him!!! The Police let him go without pressing any charges ……..typical of this country, he just laughed at me and walked off.

We never seemed to grab hold of any of the 'cream' pubs or clubs, they were all a little bit dodgy and one of the worse places was a gaff called Steelers in the middle of an estate in Bradford. I'd been in the place a few times when I was younger and even then it was a bit of an iffy manor. I always tried to put in an appearance or two in any new venues we acquired to get a feel and then get a crew settled in. We walked through the large pub to get into the club, so we could be on the till side and set up before the main doors were opened. All the punters in the boozer were shouting that we wouldn't last long and that we looked as shite as the last lot they'd had….nice drum! Believe me, there was never a dull moment in that place, two dance floors and someone always copping for a bashing. Dean and I and a guy called Alan, (Joe Ninety's brother), worked there on New Years Eve and the place was heaving, all the estate must have been in the place. The majority of the male punters were wearing suits, which all looked slightly too big, too tight, too long or just a shabby fit, I was pissing myself, someone must have robbed a shipment and sold them throughout the estate! The night went quite well, with us throwing a few clowns out for being bollocksed, until around 11.30pm, three or four guys kicked off on the dance floor and we waded in to sort them out. We gave the fuckers what for but within seconds we seemed to be fighting the whole bloody club, those close knit communities are a flaming nightmare to 'police'. We managed to get into the foyer, Alan had been well smartened up and Dean and I were getting bashed from all angles. We were squashed against the doors and because there was that many shit heads trying to land big hitters on us, we were getting away with it. The countdown for midnight started and I shouted for the foyer to be cleared as it was the New Year. To our surprise, nearly everyone went straight back into the club for the Auld Lang Syne!! One or two stayed for a 'carry on' but we spanked them and slung them out onto the cobbles, after that, it was a bother free night....crazy! We were manning a door not too far from there called the Jack and Jill pub and a hell of a lot of their punters would frequent Steelers after kick out time, so in effect, we were having to deal with quite a few of them twice. To combat the agro in J.J's, we put three quality doormen on, Big Tony, who was 25 stone, Robin, who was around 6'7" and Gary Wilson, who was tiny in comparison, 6 foot and 15 ½ stone!! Even those three weren't too happy when some clown decided he wanted to bring his pit bull dog in!! Big Tony had other commitments shortly after and left, so we brought in another Robin from the Delf Hill estate. He had a pony tail as long as your fucking arm but he was a handy fucker and a pretty decent doorman, his only problem being, that things had to done his way but that meant he had his own time schedules and kept turning up late and on a couple of occasions, he never turned up at all! Dean went down to his house to lay the law down and ended up sticking one on his chin, which down very well, causing Robin to chase Dean half way round the estate with a Samurai sword!! It was then left to yours truly to go and smooth it over with the Samurai Kid and get him to work more professionally. We managed to run both doors for a couple of years before the places closed down but we went through some good door lads.

We generally tried to have a night out with most of the door lads just before Christmas, the night had obviously to be arranged when all, or most of the guys weren't working, which was usually a Monday or a Tuesday. At that time, Steve, the gaffer at the Rio club, said he'd chauffer us around in his large Rio bus. There were around 17 of us out that night and Steve had put plenty of drink on board for us, top man. Gary had brought a few guys up from his end to make up the gang and we went round loads of boozers in the Bradford area, having a good old piss up. V.I.P's was a club in the town centre and as we pulled up outside, their doormen came out to see who the hell had turned up. I counted our boys off the bus and as I started to walk in, the big black bouncer refused me entry, saying that I was a total head case and was a magnet for agro. The owner was a Greek geezer called Peter and after a brief chat with him, I was stood at the bar with the rest of our lot. We were on our second drink, chatting with a few women that were in, when I noticed a bloke down the bar, eye balling me and pointing me out to his two mates. I've no idea who this bloke was but I'd seen him on other occasions and he'd always had a thing about having a pop at me. Low and behold he came down the bar, shouting and carrying on and then started throwing big swings at me, well, always one to oblige, I responded with a couple of shots but it was short lived and everyone jumped in to stop the, what was really a minor incident. Big black Tony, the doormen, was going mental, giving it the "I told you so" patter to his crew and the gaffer and after being refused any more service, we left. I still don't know, to this day, who the head strong guy is! Tony got shot soon after while on a door in Bradford town centre but recovered and later did some work in Cleckheaton for myself and Kinder.

We were still open for more work, if we could get in and the dosh was half decent, Gary said there was an opening in the centre of Huddersfield at Suffs Bar, so we went over to have a word with the owner, Les. He said he was having a bit of grief with some of the Town's football crew and needed a couple of good, out of town doormen. No problem, we sent him Holmsey and an Asian guy called Farrouke, both were body builders and very tasty blokes. The first night they were there, the footie crew were in and sat in the small upstairs bar. At closing time Holmsey went up to ask them to finish their drinks and leave, to which they replied "go fuck yourself" and didn't move. There was a bit of an argument and then the shit hit the fan, both doorman were at it with around a dozen Town boys, dusters, chairs and glasses were crashing into heads and bodies but when the dust settled, our two lads calmly came forward and asked what time they were required for the next night! Suff rang Gary late that night, playing fuck saying that we'd best send another two with them the next day, as there was sure to be a repeat but on a larger scale. Sure enough, when our four boys arrived, they were met by a lot bigger team and it kicked off almost straight away with our guys getting showered with bottles and glasses. The result was pretty much the same, the D.J had a bat under his decks and this was quickly made good use of as the four stood their ground. The boozer looked like a battle field Les was gutted, he rang us and told us never to send any more muscle across to his manor, as all our lot were off their heads! No pleasing some people I guess, we supplied what he'd asked for, but after a few threats, I don't think he ever opened that bar again!

The trouble with clubs and pubs is that if they aren't making the cash, they are closed or changed into a totally different business. Sometimes it's hard to acquire new doors for the staff you've got or on the other hand, it can be difficult to recruit enough good door staff to cover the doors that you've managed to grab hold of! I managed to get hold of C.J's at Morley and one in Heckmondwyke, so we pulled in more boys, Stevie and John Splading, Morgan, my brother in law Geoff, Scouse brothers Billy and Paul Hamson, Zamma. Gary had a few more guys in line from the Cleck side, so all in all, we had a good solid 'army' of decent blokes. I met a mate of mine called Tony who introduced me to yet another John who was after some graft on the doors. We met in the Bull at Clayton and after a couple of beers, we noticed a small group of guys eyeballing us across the bar. They recognised me from the Rio and after a bit of verbal, it kicked off good style. We were into them but were well outnumbered and even though we were cracking heads, we were backing up to the door area. Chairs were the only option and after a couple of these fuckers had taken the full force of a seating implement or two, we were out of there and into Tony's motor in a breath.

There were always doormen 'on the take' from the drug dealers and always some that were dealing themselves, in order to cut out the middle man. This is something that will never change and there are still plenty that involved in that seedy side of life, even in present day. One evening I was stood in the Rio foyer with Trev, when three big black guys entered. They said they were from Chapletown in Leeds and wanted to do some business. Chapletown was a predominantly 'Jamaican' area of Leeds and was well known for drug activity. The mouthpiece of the three guys said that he would send his 'soldiers' to sell their 'gear' in the club and give us nice backhander for turning a blind eye and making sure there was no competition. I told him to go fuck himself and that we weren't for sale. He wasn't too impressed with my response and pulled out his gun, threatening to' blow me away' if we didn't comply. I must say, I was 'cacking' it a bit, it's quite a daunting experience having someone point a 'shooter' at you. I stood my ground and told him again that we weren't for sale and after a lot of verbal and threats of their return, they left. Needless to say, they didn't return and shoot me! Although I did have another two encounters with fellows from Leeds that wanted a piece of anything that was going. Half a dozen came in one evening and asked if I could move any shooters for them or if we needed any and promptly opened a bag with two automatic weapons in it and a wooden box. Before I could tell them to get fucked, the box was open and on view, was a chrome '45. The second guy had a holdall which he opened, showing more pistols, some of which he said were replica guns that had been doctored to make them 'good'. I 'fobbed' them off and as we chatted, Trev said that we could make some serious dosh if we wanted to start dealing drugs and guns...........or then again.....we could end up doing plenty of bird or even getting shot down dead! For me, it was a 'no brainer'! This was a field to avoid and we stuck with the hard graft!

With the extra City & Guilds qualifications that I'd acquired, I moved into a maintenance job in the printing industry. 12 hour shifts nights and days but the money was good and the environment was decent. It was a big site (I'd worked there before, when the site was owned by Renolds.) and there were quite a lot of maintenance engineers, one of whom was Brian Pollard, a Leeds fan who I'd met through Bri Hudson on his stag night a few years earlier. There was a system there called 'The Logan's Run', which was an overhead conveyor system, which transported finished boxes of product to the large warehouses. This system worked mainly on sensors and was forever breaking down, hence, most of the engineers spent quite a lot of time repairing and 'baby sitting' it. Pollard got his foot caught in the conveyor rollers and broke his ankle and whilst he was on the 'sick', he was laid off, along with a few other engineers, due to cut backs. I was the 'lone' engineer designated to work in the large 'giftwrap' department and although the 12 hour shifts were hard but the environment wasn't bad and the work was interesting giving me a feeling of satisfaction when the setting and maintenance problems were put to bed. The company had a further plant a few miles away and I went down to have a look at a few problems, along with a guy called Resham, an Indian bloke who was electrically biased. We got on sound and he was a genuine mate who would go out of his way to help you. We were working on a large piece of machinery that needed part of it lifting up with a forklift truck to gain access. Whilst working on the underside, the thing slipped and as it crashed to the floor with an almighty bang, it had actually hit me on the side of the head, the neck, the chest and thigh, ripping part of my overall clean off. I was bleeding form various cuts and scrapes but unbelievably still standing in the same spot. I looked across to Resham saying "fuck me mate, that was close, if I'd had time to realise what was happening, I'd have shit myself!!". He just stood there looking like he was going to cry before blurting out that I was bleeding and started running round like a headless chicken! It wasn't as bad as it looked, although it did cause a halt in production with half the workforce rushing to see what had occurred. We did call it a draw for the day and laughed at how close I was to getting crushed under a ton of cast iron! I still have the scar on my neck to remind me of how close I was to being 'levelled'!

My daughter started ice skating down at the city's ice rink and took to it like a duck to water; she passed everything in a breath and was soon ready for small competitions. I soon found out that this sport was a massive drain on the monetary side on anybody's resources, so there was no let up on the work aspect of mine or my wife's lives. Lucy was winning almost every skating competition that she entered, which was fantastic but the cost was escalating at a rapid rate. Coaching fees, arena costs, skating boots, costumes, travelling fees, the cutting and editing of music skating programs, gym costs, overnight accommodation when away in competitions and all the other bits and bats, crikey, the list was never ending!

I was doing at least two nights a week on the doors sometimes three! with a hell of a lot of organising thrown in for good measure and working up to 70 hours on the maintenance. The maintenance was sound, I was well on top of what I was doing, and the manager of the department was a lad called Sean, who was commuting from Harwood, Blackburn. Sean is a season ticket holder at Rovers and still goes to a hell of a lot of Blackburn's games, we bonded well and have been really good friends ever since. Leeds were playing at Ewood Park in a midweek game so myself and another good mate that I worked with in the print, Sean Gorman, said we would go to the match and stop at Sean's house. Gorman is a fucking Man U fan but to be fair, loves football and knows his stuff where the glorious game is concerned. It was a truly eventful game with Blackburn's keeper getting sent off, Rovers leading by a goal and Leeds equalising towards the end. We were sat on the front row of the stand and as soon as Leeds levelled, I jumped up and was dancing at the back of the linesman, with Gorman shouting at me to sit down. I turned round to face the stand and realised what he meant, half the fans were stood up all going barmy and pointing at my good self, a few police and stewards were into the crowd trying to calm them down and as I returned quickly to my seat, Gorman said, "You'll cause a riot, you looney Leeds twat!". We went for beers with a lot of Sean's mates and they were sound, I've been and stayed with him in Blackburn quite a few times and have always been accepted in their circles, good bunch of guys.

Christmas on the horizon and Kinder and I arranged a coach to take some of the lads to Wakefield on the beer, the Monday night before Santa's busy day. We arrived in Wakefield and were straight on the piss in the town centre, we were 18 strong and full of the festive spirit. The night was going great and we made our way up to Roof Top Gardens nightclub at around 10.30 pm. In we went, through the large glass fronted foyer and into the main bar area where we all got drinks and then started to drift around the number of bars and dance floors. We'd been in about an hour and I was stood at the main bar with Geoff, three of our guys were having a bit of an argument with four local lads towards the main foyer doors, so we moved over to calm the situation. These lads were stating we weren't local and didn't belong on their patch and as I tried to explain that we weren't there for a rumble, another guy came from behind them and landed a small stool straight in the right hand side of my 'boat'. I hit the floor in what seemed to be slow motion, I quickly shook my head and covered up as the boots came in. the balloon went up and it spilled through the door, straight into the main foyer. I picked myself up and followed the fracas, a huge bouncer came at me as I went through the door and he had dusters on both hands. I landed one on the guy but it didn't appear to make any impact whatsoever and he was hitting everyone in punching distance. This seemed to be a planned attack on us, there were approximately ten door staff and around seven local guys and they were all wading into our crew, who were now all in the foyer. The Wild West saloons had nothing on this 'ruck', it was pandemonium with blood splattered blokes who all appeared to be fighting for their lives. A couple of doormen were out for the count on the deck but the huge guy was still banging away at anything that moved, I was hung around his neck but it was as though I was a winter scarf! Now Geoff is no slouch when it comes to it and is as hard as they come but when this big bloke hit him, he lifted him clean off the floor, his broken frame sliding down the wall and onto the carpet in a heap, there just didn't seem to be any way of stopping this bloke. Someone smashed the till over his bonce and that slowed him up before he got a glass smashed into his neck and reluctantly threw the towel in, with the red stuff pouring out of him. There were a few local boys throwing glasses and ashtrays from the steps and as we moved towards them, they legged it to the top level and each time we attempted to reach them, they showered us with bar stools. Trev and Stevie Spod had been thrown through the doors and were laid half battered on the pavement outside, the opposite side of the road was covered with a couple of hundred punters that were watching the 'show' through the large foyer windows. The riot cops arrived with crash hats and shields and the situation was quickly defused, phone calls were made and our coach turned up on the scene. The police had most of our lads outside and were trying to get us all on board the coach but it kicked off again, as a few of our guys were still inside and we weren't moving without them. Two ambulances arrived and the big bloke, who still had shards of glass in his neck, was brought out, along with a couple of doormen and two or three local geezers. The big bloke still managed to throw a punch into big Gary's head as the law intervened and was then put in one of the ambulances. I definitely didn't want to see him again in a hurry! We were all aboard the 'skylark' and escorted out of town and sent in the direction of Bradford. A couple of skirmishes broke out on the bus between the lads, resulting in a lot off slagging off regarding who had held their own and who hadn't but it all got put to bed. Geoff had a broken eye socket and broken ribs, Stevie had broken ribs and a broken hand, Trev had broken ribs and plenty of others had a string of injuries but the plus factor being that of us were sat in the ambulances or the cells.

I got dropped off at a curry house with Scouse Paul, Stevie and his brother John and ordered some fodder, it was only when I went to the pisser that I realised I wasn't in the best of health. I inspected my wounds in the mirror, a large open wound on my cheek and my eye lid was split clean in half, so much that when I pulled it down, I could still see through it! Cancel the food then and it was off to the hospital for us all to get sorted out. At the infirmary, Geoff was already there, receiving treatment for his injuries. We all had a giggle, especially when John (who had got the curry guys to 'bag' his food) pulled out his supper and started to stuff his face in the casualty area.! To say the hospital staff weren't too pleased is definitely an understatement!!

The wife went ballistic but hell, I didn't cause my injuries or start any of the bother that had occurred, sometimes it's just fate, wrong place, wrong time. I went into work and Gorman was over the moon that he hadn't accepted the invitation to come along on the night out. Two week later, I recall working on the door at CJ's in Morley on New Years Eve with Geoff and we were obviously still well 'marked'. A group of four guys came in and as they passed us to walk down the stairs, I heard one say, "Fuck me, I wouldn't mess with those two" and his mate replied, "I wouldn't want to meet the other fuckers that marked 'em!'.

A few months later and the shit hit the fan yet again. The two lads that were working on the door at C.J's in Morley for us, Morgan and John, disappeared. I had to rearrange bodies on different doors to fill in the gaps and try to find out where the hell they'd buggered off to. Everyone knew that there had been a shooting and a murder at the Raggalds pub up in Queensbury on the edge of Bradford and apparently Morgan and John were in the frame. After supposedly hiding out in Kent and then over in Tenneriffe, the two were picked up by the law, locked up and grilled. Drugs, money, guns, turf wars, gang wars, or just plain greed more often than not, all lead to a sorry end for most. More often than not, most people involved in those categories end up on the losing side of life. To this day, there a few different versions of what actually happened at the Raggalds and I'd rather not enlighten you all to my version of what went down that night. The true facts that can't be changed are that Michael Briggs was shot dead and Bainesy and John Paisley were also shot and injured and John Spalding and Morgan Duffy both got life for the events of that night. I went to see John in Armley prison and it was a though he was referring to a third party rather than himself and maintained that he was set up and that he wasn't even there. A lot of other people, plus forensics, told a different tale.

Last game of the season that year for Leeds was away at Spurs and my brother Bryan had sorted us a box out through work and the brewery guy. Quality! Eight of us went down to White Hart Lane and as we pulled up in the players car park outside the front of the club, all the fans were waving and cheering at us!!?? Fucking sad tossers! We were 'suited and booted' and sat in the lounge with plenty to drink, watching the Formula 1 on the large screen. The box we had was smack bang on the half way line, arguably the best view in the house! We dined and drank plenty and then got down to the match. Out of the sides of the box, we could more or less see the full length of the pitch and we were giving the 'thumbs up' to the 'Home' fans, ha. The box to our left had a team of 'boys' in it and they were less than impressed when we started to cheer on the 'Mighty Whites'! ha ha. MOT….(Marching on Together) to those of you that aren't very well educated.! Our waitress for the day did us proud and kept us fed and watered throughout and we all hit the roof when Leeds equalised to get a draw from the game. We got plenty of abuse from all sides as we celebrated, ha, objects were being thrown at the glass and "cut throat" gestures were in abundance. At the final whistle, I grabbed half a crate of 'Bud' and headed for the 'likely lads' in the next box. I was ready for a set too or a beer or two, whatever their choice. I steamed in and said, "Good game lads, fancy a bear?". Two or three of them told me to get fucked off and the rest had beers and a bit of a chat. Nobody got bashed, so all ended well and an hour later we were heading home.

I had stopped going down to London for the Wembley rugby final weekend and instead had taken to trips to Dublin. The Lord Clyde pub on the outskirts of Bradford town centre was a place that Gorman and myself played pool for. I'd been a regular in there for a few years and could relax without fear of some clown that I'd bashed on a door turning up looking for revenge. The gaff was and Irish boozer and was run by Sean Dwyer, a big 20 odd stone Bradford City fan. Sean was a sound bloke, gave and took plenty of banter and was a good old laugh and decent mate (for a City fan!!) he ribbed me no end after one Monday night when Gorman had taken a right liberty with me. We'd been having the 'crack' all evening and when I was sat on a small bar stool chatting, the cheeky bastard hit me in the side of the chin from behind. I was off the stool and on the floor and even though I was up in an instant, Gorman was out of the door and fifty yards up the road before you could fart! I say he took a liberty because we are such good mates, he knew that once I'd seen the funny side of it, he knew that he wouldn't be getting a slap and he was right. One evening we were playing pool when there was a slight commotion at the bar and Sean asked me if I knew the guy causing the stir. It was a bloke called Steve Hume, whom I'd met quite a few times since we'd been in our teens. He threatened to smash the bar up if Sean served him bottles of warm 'Pils', so the situation was easily sorted and Steve became a regular in the Clyde. Over the years we all meet really handy fellows but in my opinion Steve Hume was 'pound for pound', the handiest around in the Bradford area during the nineties. We've had the odd 'difference of opinion' but never fallen out and although he can be a volatile fucker when it suits him, I'll always have plenty of time for him. I spent a lot of time in that pub in the nineties and made a lot of pals. Gorman, Sean Dwyer, Wolfey, Tommy Brumf, , Rob, Paddy, Shouey, Jack, Steve, John, Paddy, Darren, Les, old Brian and Peter Preistley (who tragically died form a knife wound to the chest), to name a few.

The first Dublin trip I went on with the Clyde lads was tremendous. It was always on the same weekend as the Irish Hurling final, so Dublin was at a complete standstill with supporters. The final was on the Sunday afternoon, so because of the pub opening laws, the landlords would just lock the places up and it didn't matter whether you were in or out, the doors stayed locked. Everyone just got totally bollocksed and the atmosphere was brilliant. The Clyde trip returned home on the Monday but that particular year, I stayed on and went down south with Gorman, Dwyer and old

Rob. We had a car over the next five days, went to Mountmellick, Tullamore and Portlaoise. The hotel in Mountmellick had a large public bar on the side and with the amount of booze we sank in there, it's a wonder we ever made it home. Sean Gorman's family are from Tullamore and when we arrived on the main street, it appeared totally dead. We heard music form the main club and entered to find Gorman's gran dancing on the table to howls and cheers from a half full concert room. Apparently, we'd arrived in the middle of a funeral wake!!! There were major family arguments centred around who was going to put us up, feed us and buy our drinks.......we didn't really have much say in the matter, fantastic people. The Dublin trips lasted three or four years for me and were all great times, we were always booked into the Wynns Hotel which was right in the middle of the city. The second trip I went on was the most eventful. Sean Gorman and I had been invited into a wedding 'bash' at the hotel by a couple of Irish 'lookers' that we'd been chatting to at the main bar. We were getting on fine and being introduced to a few of the wedding party, when this big drunken bruiser suddenly accused me of stealing his wallet!!! There were a few punches thrown and we ended up being surrounded by a large group of irate, well under the influence big Irish blokes. The outcome being that I let the brides father quicly search me and put the matter to bed. Hence to say, the apologies were non stop and we didn't buy another drink! On the same trip, I was thrown out of a club after a slight altercation with another local bloke and ended up back at the hotel around midnight. Big Sean Dwyer and Rob were in the bar, along with some guys who were there for some kind of Shop Stewards Convention.

Among this group were a young bouncer form Waterford (whom I'd met earlier), a Chelsea fan, a QPR fan, a couple of Villa lads and a another guy. You could tell that the football guys had all been 'boys' in their time and we were having a good laugh whilst reliving our football stories. The bar shut and the porters were left with the job of supplying us with our drinks. We'd all had plenty and were getting on well, apart from the QPR bloke, who for some reason, the more drink he had, the more sly quips he was throwing in my direction. Things came to a head and I told the arsehole to back up his comments and have a piece of me or to fuck off to bed. I stood up and fired a couple of combinations into him, whereupon, his arse just fell out. As he staggered backwards, he mumbled something about Leeds fans being fucking animals and hastily buggered off towards his room, without me having to give a proper bashing!

I had half a day off the booze, while I visited the historic Kilmainham Jail. The building was built in 1796 and held the majority of the leaders of the Irish rebellions through to its decommissioning in 1924. A truly deep insight into the political history of Ireland was shown on film and a tour of the prison gave an in depth view of the conditions that the prisoners endured. Quite a few movies have had scenes filmed at the prison, with the most known film being The Italian Job in 1969. Most of the guys thought I was a bit of a loon for visiting the place but there's nothing wrong with a bit of further education.

There never seemed to be a dull moment around this time of my life, we were forever going to have words with people over owed monies or for being out of line with third parties, all par for the course when you mixed in the circles that we did. A family matter meant a visit to see a quite volatile, big in his field, influential drug dealer. Over the years, I'd been to visit quite a few people, for various reasons and 8a.m. is more often than not, a very good time to turn up. The dealer, let's call him Vic, was a guy that I'd met a year earlier, so I knew what to expect when we arrived at his manor. My two brothers and Gary in tow, I knocked on the door and when it opened, I pushed my way in, telling a bleary eyed Vic to put the kettle on. Gary said he needed a piss and went straight upstairs for a quick 'once over' to make sure the place wasn't full of 'back up'. We were well tooled up, just to be on the safe side and if the shit had really hit the fan, someone was going to end up shot. Vic knew the score and new he was on a loser. There was some of Vic's gear to drop off and a wedge to pick up. After a 'brew' and a 'smoke', all ends were tied up and owed monies paid. Vic gave a knowing grin as we bid him farewell. Everybody happy, no injuries or damage and business concluded.

I decided to have a break and take a decent holiday with the family. So Sue, Lucy and my niece Emma, Russ's daughter, went to Los Angeles in the States. A week in L.A, which incorporated passes into Disney Land and a rake of other stuff. Absolutely brilliant, the kids loved it, all the rides and shows at Disney were superb and the hospitality shown by the Yanks was second to none. On arrival at Disney Land, the security staff pulled us to one side and informed us of the security measures that were in place regarding child abduction, they were really on the ball with reference to that and advised us not to let the children out of our sight for one second, as they could be lifted, re-dressed and taken out of the premises in a matter of minutes. That scared the hell out of us, I got a bit of a phobia about it and was eye balling everyone, wondering if they were kiddy snatchers! That aside, we had a great week there and visited the Universal Studios, Hollywood and a host of other attractions, then drove through the desert, over to Las Vegas. Driving through that red hot desert was a bit of ordeal but it's definitely worth it when you first catch sight of the buildings of Vegas shimmering in the sunlight, it's like some kind of oasis that just seems to appear out o nowhere.

We were booked into the Luxor hotel (the giant pyramid), a real eye opener of a building but then again, the majority of the hotel/casino's there are all stunning pieces of architecture. I made a point of visiting the Flamingo Hilton, which was one of the first hotels to be built there and was opened in 1946 as the Pink Flamingo. The opening of the hotel/casino was the start of a casino boom in Vegas, it was the brain child of gangster, Benjamin (Bugsy) Siegel but because he over shot the budget agreed with the mob bosses, it cost him his life.

All the hotels/casinos, on the strip had shows on outside, which were there to entice the public into the casinos. On entering the hotels, you have to walk through the casino, even to reach the reception and although children are allowed to pass through the casinos, if they stop for any reason at all, the security staff are there in a breath to move them on. You can literally smell the money and the sound of fruit machines paying out is almost deafening, there are large turntables with top of the range vehicles on them as prizes for crap or bingo games, it's an almost mesmerising atmosphere. The security in the Luxor was quite tight, there were staff on the stairwells and in the lifts, no access was given to either unless a room key was shown as proof of hotel residency.

Underneath all the glitz and glamour, I found Vegas to be quite a seedy place really, throughout the day people would be pushing porn advert leaflets into your hand, even though you had young kids on your arm. That aside, I would recommend a visit to Vegas, to anyone who has yet to step foot on the sands of one of the richest resorts in the world. When the sun goes down and the 'strip' lights up, it is without doubt, a different world, there is entertainment outside each and everyone of the hotels, which is, of course there to entice the punters into the large casinos. The most interesting attraction at the time for myself, was the show outside the Treasure Island hotel. A large galleon ship manned by a team of pirates, floated around a man made lagoon in the grounds of the hotel and into a purposely built harbour. They were met by a small army of Red Coats that was situated in the cliffs of the harbour and the set too between the two groups was tremendous. The galleon was eventually sunk and the pirate raid was thwarted after a twenty minute battle that included plenty of musket fire and the odd cannon booming out. The galleon was then raised from the depths and returned to its starting position, ready for the next show......quality entertainment!

The Grand Canyon is one of the wonders of the world and we decided to pay the place a visit and see it in all its splendour. We took a trip on a seven seater plane, over the Hoover Dam and all the way through the canyon before landing at a small air strip above the massive gorge. There was a meal laid on and then we were treated to a film showing on huge Imax cinema screen. We toured all the way round the top of the canyon and the purpose built museum, before doing some shopping in the large retail centre that has been erected there. The weather became overcast and there was a bit of panic generated from a few of the pilots on the air strip, the pilot flying our small plane decided to brave the storm, so we boarded and got ready to head back to Vegas. The pilots of the other half dozen planes thought it was in the best interests of the passengers to stay put until the storm had run it's course. I was sat up front next to the pilot, with Sue, Lucy and Emma seated behind me and then three German guys seated at the back of the plane. The turbulence was quite bad and we would have been thrown all over the place if it wasn't for the fact that we were well strapped in. The sky was black, visibility very poor and the small plane was being tossed all over, we were almost upside down on several occasions. Each time a small pocket of light appeared through the blackness, the pilot headed towards it, only to be engulfed in total darkness before reaching it. Beads of sweat were dripping from the pilot's forehead as he tried in vain to fly the small plane through the storm and I could tell that the panic element related to this traumatic ordeal was beginning to get the better of him. A constant barrage of pleading and begging with ground control to find him a route around the terrible storm seemed to be in vain then, low and behold, the sky seemed to open up and a huge bright light appeared, opening a tunnel of vision up for us and our ordeal was coming to an end. We flew straight down the beam of light and towards the red hot skies above Las Vegas.

We landed safely and a huge grin on his face, the pilot handed us a certificate, stating that we were never in danger and thanked us for flying with the airway. I know for a fact that the geezer was shitting it! The rest of the planes from the small airfield arrived for touchdown approximately 5 hours later, so I was quite pleased that our pilot had taken the bull by the horns and battled his way through, although, I can honestly say that I was glad to be back on solid ground.

Before we left the Luxor Hotel, Sue had spotted a 'very' nice jewellery store in the Hotel and the credit card was flexed to accommodate (that girl did love her gold and diamonds).

The American hospitality is second to none, although at first I did think that they were taking the piss in the way that they address you. It's in you face from day one, with all that 'how you doing?' and 'hey, how's your day? Even so, I was impressed with how everyone seemed to bend over backwards and tried to help with anything they could.

Reality soon set in as soon as we were back on British soil. When I went to fill the car up at a petrol station near Heathrow airport, it was a case of "What pump are you at?" and then they mutter the price at you without a please, thank you or a fuck off! The majority of youngsters that serve us in this country, even up to present day, seem to have a, 'couldn't care less attitude'.

A couple of months later, I was in the office at work being told that since I had got a decent hold on the maintenance schedules in the 'giftwrap' department, the production levels were up by over 30 percent and they were thinking of updating some of the 'unwind' machines.The unwind machines in the main production area were mainly German 'Moller' machines and American 'Elsner' machines. The one's in question were the Elsner machines, which came from Hanover in Pensylvania U.S.A. A trip was arranged for Gorman, who was chief 'setter' in the Giftwrap department,

Resham Singh, the electrician and myself. We were trusted to go to Hanover and access the new design of the 'unwind' machine that was being produced by Elsner and report back our findings as to whether the new design would be beneficial to future production in the Giftwrap department.

We arrived at Newark airport and met by the 'rep' and a large Lincoln Cadillac, which, with the three of us in the back, had acres of room to spare!! We were taken to a large diner situated off the beaten track, where we had a few beers and a decent meal before being dropped off at our Motel. It was a Black Ball 8 Motel with a huge fat bloke behind the counter, who spoke in 'yes', 'no' answers. We got freshened up and headed a couple of blocks to the nearest bar, which was a 'pizza' type place with a dozen big 'Rigs' parked outside. Now, if you picture this place as being similar to the television program 'Northern Exposure', with plenty of 20 stone bearded blokes driving round with rifles and dead stags in the back of their trucks, then you're somewhere on the right lines.

We entered the bar and all the big bearded truckers went quiet and stared in our direction, Sean mumbled "fucking hell Dave", to which I giggled and shouted to 'skirt' behind the bar "3 large beers please love." Now all the huge guys at the bar were drinking half pints, quite a funny set, those Yanks, so the barmaid had to root about a bit to find us some pint glasses. We 'downed' them quite sharpish and ordered another round, to which the barmaid "I'll get you a pitcher, that'll be cheaper, if you take a seat, I'll bring one over." We got settled and started to watch the American Football that was starting on the large screen, as a couple of these huge truckers came over and wanted to know where we were from and how many pints we drank and the rest. They were 'gobsmacked' when we said we could easily drink 10 or 12 pints of this stuff in a sitting, hence we had a good evening, chatting with these guys about all kinds.

Over the next three days, we made our reports and spoke on the phone regarding changes to the new 'unwind' prototype. Teething problems aside, the three of us thought that the purchase of at least two of the machines would be beneficial to our production, so that in mind, we finished off and home went.

Christmas was round the corner and everything went smoothly for once, with myself and Kinder managing to accommodate all 'our' pubs and clubs with doorstaff but life rarely runs smoothly and it was a turbulent year that lay ahead.

January '96, a bleak foggy Monday morning and I was asked to go the airport to pick up the Yank engineer from Elsner. There was no company vehicle available, so I had to go in my own Merc 190E, which, at the time was my pride and joy. He got settled in and later I dropped him at his hotel, which was on my way home. Monday night, myself and Sean Gorman were off down to the Lord Clyde for our pool league, the American declined our offer of a night out and so I arranged to pick him up the next morning. It was a cold morning and the fog was still really thick in patches, Gorman didn't answer the door, so I went to the Hotel and picked up the American. We headed a couple of mile to the factory and unfortunately I went across a 'T' junction in the fog, there was a footpath and I braked to guide the front of the car into the opening but hit the lamp that jutted out. I went through the windscreen and then through the side window as the car slammed to a halt. I reversed the car out and parked on the side of the road, I was bleeding from quite a few wounds and when the Yank said he'd hurt his hand and would have to put a claim in, I told him we were on company time, so the claim would have to go through them. I ended up at a friend's house not too far from the factory and woke up in the afternoon!!! I went to the hospital to get 'fixed' up and treated for concussion.

Now there are quite a few different opinions as to what exactly happened on that day. The incident was only a hundred yards from the factory and apparently, I went into the works, whereupon one of the 'jobsworths' working on the security gate, rang the law, who turned up with three motors and around ten 'uniforms'. According to most, I just wondered off in a daze, others said I went off the premises in the boot of a car to avoid the law, as I was probably under the influence and others say I just 'legged' it over the back fence! I was suspended from work while enquiries were made. Now my employers, stated that I had advised the American engineer to make a fraudulent claim against the company, as they thought that any injury claim for him should have been made against my vehicle insurance. The lad actually should have been looked after by company and covered by company insurance on entering the U.K, so I asked them if he was covered by them when I'd picked him up from the airport in company time, (albeit, in my own vehicle). They appeared to be 'bricking' it for not covering all angles and were desperately needing a scapegoat...........yours truly!! They were adamant that I had to leave my position, so they could save face and agreed to pay me everything that I was entitled to, as if I had resigned. I new that if I didn't accept the terms, it would just be a matter of time before they removed me from the position for other reasons that they could come up with………Adios!! It came to my attention that a couple of directors had had their say and made it clear that the book was stopping with me, one in particular, had supposedly said that I was just a hired thug (because of the door connections) and that the company was well shut of me. I'll refrain from naming the guy. Statements such as he made though aren't forgotten easily.

I was working out at the gym quite a bit then and Nick, the owner, was a builder, so I went and gave him a hand for a few weeks while I was between jobs. On a night I was well into the doors, which was doing ok, with around ten 'manors' on the go and a good 40 bodies on call. At tat time we had the ponytail and waistcoat brigade, Piotre, a Polish guy was well into bodybuilding and sported a long ponytail and black leather waistcoat. Ponytail Mark was very similar in attire and size, he was quite a clever kid and worked for the council. Rishtu was another foreign mate of Piotre's, he was bald but did the bodybuilding and waistcoat thing. These lads were damn good doormen when it suited them but weren't too keen on moving form one club once they had their feet under the table. A young lad called Jay was on the scene, big lad, ponytail and looked the part but I always feel that he held back and seemed quite apprehensive, although I did persevere with him and tried to groom him, rightly some say, others not. Others in the frame then were, Richie, a big set, really well mannered Jamaican kid called Simon, Chris, John, Garfy, Roger, Jamie………to mention a few.

There was one evening around that time at the Rio when Bob was having a bit a verbal do with some arsehole and Bob basically told him that he was on his last chance and would be out o his ear if he had to speak to him again. As Bob turned to walk away, the twat hit him with two glasses, one either side of his head! Bob was sorted out at the hospital and his injuries weren't as bad as originally thought. In that game, there's always some arsehole wanting to do the doormen some serious damage. Bob was soon fixed up and back on the job.

I'd got another 'day' job with a Lift and Escalator firm, Gregson & Bell, which wasn't brilliant but it brought in a few quid and would have to do for the time being. A Bradford firm got in touch with me regarding a 'setting' job that they needed sorting out abroad. The firm were an agent for American Elsner machines in the UK and they did a lot of business with Fine Arts. Their problem being was that they didn't have an engineer that could set up the A4 Elsner unwind machine, so one of the directors from Fine Arts, who'd been involved with me in reference to the Giftwrap department, had told them I was the boy they needed to speak to. A top chap from the company rang and offered me £2000 plus expenses to go to Saudi and set up a couple of A4 Elsners for them, to which I replied, "no problem, as long as you give me full time employment when I get back." He was having none of it, maybe due to rumours regarding my departure from Fine Arts, or not, who can say? It was no secret that all the top top Brass from both firms were chums and I've no doubt that the incident had been discussed. I couldn't just up sticks and go because of the 'Lift' job I'd just started, so after three days of this bloke ringing me, I finally gave him a resounding NO...... I thought it was his loss, without a doubt.

I followed quite a bit of boxing at that time and could tell you, the majority of the title holders, the best pound for pound fighters and what was happening in the fight game. We were on a race day out to Haydock Park with a full coach load from the Clyde, Sean was on the trip with his mate John from Harwood and we had a 'ball'. On the same day, Nigel Benn was fighting Steve Collins for the World title. My luck was in and I was taking quite a few quid from the course bookies......celebrating with plenty of beers in the course bar! From the course we headed to a large boozer near Warrington, where we had booked to eat beforehand. We'd all had a good day out and the night was going champion until the Benn fight. Benn was never my cup of tea and I had never put a bean on him to win........until his first fight with Collins! I had a flutter with half a dozen of the guys on our trip and when Benn packed in, most of my horse winnings went for a nose-dive! I lost it for a couple of minutes and in return for the heavy verbal I was getting from our lads, I turned a couple of tables over in the boozer! Everyone was covered in booze and going mental, shouting that I'd gone round the bend. Needless to say, I had to apologise profusely to the landlord and his staff and offer to pay for the broken glasses etc. I also had to replace the lad's drinks that I'd flattened! There was three hours to kill before we headed home, so a few of us made our way into Warrington town centre. We had a decent drink and a few laughs but there was a bit of an altercation at the taxi rank and three or four local scrotums got a slap. We were back to coach pick up point with time to spare and after waiting for a straggler or two, we were on our way back to Bradford. On the way back, most of the lads were catching a few 'zzz's' but there were a few in a more boisterous mode that were knocking out a tune or two. There were three or four younger Leeds fans half way down the coach, two of which were Andy Gorman and Steve Hardy and they decided to start belting out a few footie tunes, which was fine until they started with the Munich air disaster and the Bradford City fire. There were quite a few City fans on board and even though they were out for the count, the songs were out of order, so I asked the guys to curb it and stick to 'normal' tunes. I was told that I was an 'old school' Leeds fan and they were the new breed and I should shut the fuck up and sit back in my seat. As we were expressing differences of opinion, one of the lads, Steve, said that he was going to come and shut me up and put me in my place and he started towards the back seat with Andy coming up behind him. This was something I seriously didn't need but I had no choice than to stop him in his tracks with a straight right to the gob. The punch knocked him backwards and although he took it, he was shaken and sounded off with a volley of 'fucks'. There was quite a lot of loud verbal going on and whole of the bus was now awake. I myself was getting a right earful from all corners for ruining the day from waking sleepers who had no idea what had happened. The commotion calmed and everyone took their seats and I recall Sean's mate John saying something about Leeds fans being 'unhinged' to the point that they scrap among themselves! Back at the Clyde, the 'afters' were going on well into the early hours and I was still getting slated off, so to ease the earache, I stood on a chair and apologised to everyone for my actions and although there were few who knew what had gone on, I left it at that. It was a couple of weeks later that the facts came out and then I was the one receiving all the apologies and everyone was saying that the 'songs' were well out of order. Oh well..........if you can take the criticism.....you can definitely accept the praises! I've had beers with Steve and Andy a few times since that night and they're sound, decent guys. Too much ale sometimes dulls our senses and can cause some major problems in our lives. We all tend to step out of line from time to time but it's being able to admit it, stand up and take the consequences of our actions and being able to move on, that brings out the man in us.

Shortly after, Blackburn Sean, had arranged to stay at mine so we could have a few beers and when he'd finished work, we met up in the Lord Clyde. Tim Nixon, who also worked at Fine Arts and who I've mentioned from the scooter days, also turned up. Now, I'd heard that Tim had been bad mouthing me, saying that a lad called John Pickles had been dismissed, in connection with my 'car crash' incident and it was my fault. I quickly pulled Tim in order to sort things out and he apologised, stating he'd been out of order. We had a good drink and the three of us headed up to the Rio club. Yorkey, big Richard, Baz and a couple of others were on the door and after a brief chat, we were at the bar. The place was full of skinheads and punks, as the bands were playing their stuff. We made our way round to the small bar and I turned round to see Tim butt this big skinhead, opening his nose and sitting him on his arse! He explained that the guy had moved towards Sean, hand raised and had no doubt that he was about to land one on him! We were surrounded by around 30 of these clowns and being bombarded with beer cans and plastic glasses, along with a torrid volley of insults. The bottom bar is around a corner, so it isn't in full view of the whole club, can be slightly secluded and has only exit as such. The policy of the club at that time, was plastic glasses and tins only but in some cases the barstaff would serve females their drinks in a glass, at their own if they thought fit to do so. Personally,

I thought that the same rule should apply to all but on this occasion, I was glad it didn't.

This mob were edging toward us and weren't far short of frothing at the mouth!! There was nobody else in the vicinity, apart from a young couple next to the bar and they just froze, petrified. The young girl had a tall glass tumbler next to her and I quickly made a grab for it and lunged toward the nearest skinhead, after smashing it on a table. I grabbed the guy and held the glass against his chin shouting to his mates to back off or he'd lose his chin. I edged down the bar toward the opening with Sean and Tim tucked in behind me and we made our way toward the foyer, making sure to hold this ringleader between myself and this sizeable crew of wannabe's. The doormen came from all over and were all shouting and wanting to know what the hell was going on. As we entered the foyer, I gave this guy a right hook that sent him to his knees and told the door lads the basics of what had happened, Sean 'lamped' another 'skin', who was pushing into the foyer and we were out of there, down the steps, into a cab and back to the Clyde.

The following week, I was working at the Rio and a couple of those involved were 'eyeballing' me but there were no repercussions. Not all the skinhead lads that frequented the place were 'wrong uns', there were three young skins that used to come and watch all kinds of bands, one was called Gary and he often came over for a chat. One evening though, there was a Battle of the Bands event on and the 'drum' was full of rockers when the three skins came in. One of the bar staff said she'd heard a group of lads at the bar saying that they were going to 'do' the three lads. The place was packed so I told the three lads to make themselves scarce for their good. They weren't too happy about it really but after a bit of persuasion, they agreed to leave, so I let them out of the back door. Five minutes later, the girl on the front till was shouting in the foyer that there was some bother outside. Trev and Bob were stood on the steps but didn't want get involved with anything outside the premises, as we'd been warned by 'plod' before. I could see a taxi on the forecourt, surrounded by long haired yobs in 'leathers' and the driver stood a few yard away with his head in his hands. There was one yob in the front of the cab throwing punches into the back at one of the young skins and the other two skins were half in and half out of the car getting the shit kicked out of them from all angles by a dozen or so other rockers. I ran down the steps, much to Trev and Bob's dismay, who were saying to wait for the law but I seriously think it would have been disastrously too late to do so. I easily decked two or three of these 'long hairs' and screamed at them to have a go with someone who was at least capable of having a pop back. I dragged the wanker out of the front seat and butted him, dropping him onto his shitter and told the driver to get back in the fucking car. I lifted the battered lads into the car, they were in a sorry state and one was unconscious, they were covered in blood. The odd rocker boy was edging closer and they were all giving it plenty of verbal but each time I fronted them, they backed up and none made a move…..tough lot eh!!? I told the driver to get them to the hospital, quick as poss and he drove off.

Trev said that if the group had made a move on me, him and Bob would have been straight in but that I still shoudn't have got involved. Inside the club, a couple of the 'heroes' were 'larging' it at the bar saying what a great fight they'd just had, I made this guy look about two foot tall in front of his audience and them threw him out. Young Gary, the skinhead came to see me a few weeks after to thank me but I didn't see him or his mates much after that night.

There was some kind of 'fall out' with a couple of doormen and the gaffer at a place called 42nd Street in Bradford, a 'drum' that was known for a bit of fisty cuffs (and the rest!). I got a phone call asking if we would cover the door there, as the bouncers had walked out. Ponytail Mark and Piotre covered the place on the Friday night but I needed them to cover the Saturday night as well and although I rang them both constantly throughout the whole of Saturday, I couldn't get hold of them. One of the guys told me that neither of them were happy at being placed at the 42nd and were keeping their heads down so they wouldn't have to repeat the chor! The fuckers left me high and dry and I had to pull in a couple of extra boys in from elsewhere. I went down to work the 42nd Street myself and took Scouser Paul with me as my 'second'. All seemed to be going well until a gang of known faces turned up on the door. In this team of around fifteen guys, were names such as Daniels, Trotter and Colemans. All known names to any streetwise bloke and of course, the law. Now some of these lads were good guys but definitely a hand full when they were in the mood. Gervais has since passed away but he and my mate Gary had a chat and a good laugh about the incident later.

We let them in a couple at a time, so they could pay at the desk but I turned to see it kick off, after a couple of them decided not to pay. Paul was adamant that they were all to pay, no matter who they were and he was having a set too with a guy called Timmy Trotter. I'd been introduced to Timmy in the past;- in prison and a couple of times in Bradford town and always thought he was sound, buy this was different ground, as we were trying to do a job. After the fists and boots had been exchanged, Paul had a good hold and was not letting go of the lad. I persuaded him it was a good idea to release his grip, taking into consideration that we were surrounded by the large group who were by now all holding beer glasses and threatening to cut us up! They all moved to the bar area and still decided to launch a 'nice' volley of pint pots in our direction, covering us in small cuts and stale booze!! A couple of phone calls later and I had a few boys in there as back up but this wasn't all in black and white. There were more of this crew turning up by the minute and it was said that they were tooled with shivs (and the rest). So because this was all to do with the dispute between the landlord and the doormen who'd walked out, we decided to leave them to it rather than get ourselves dragged into a potential war that was really nothing to do with us.

Photo texts:-

My brilliant nan.

Mum & dad.

With Linds in Dubai

Dodgy speedos

Linds with the little soldier.

Proud dad.

One of many scars

Me & Russ with Mr Eubank

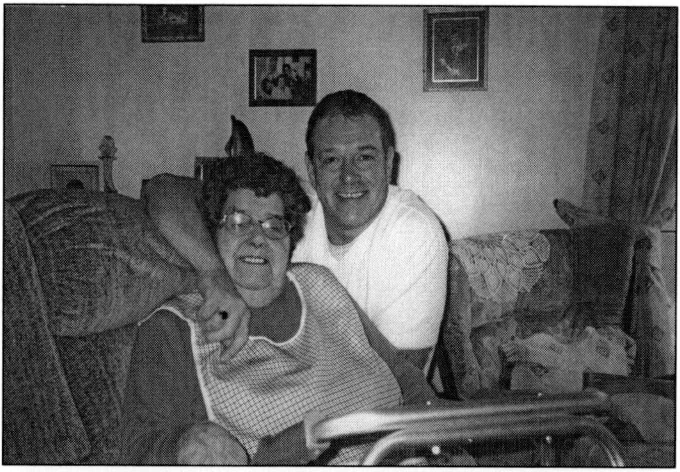

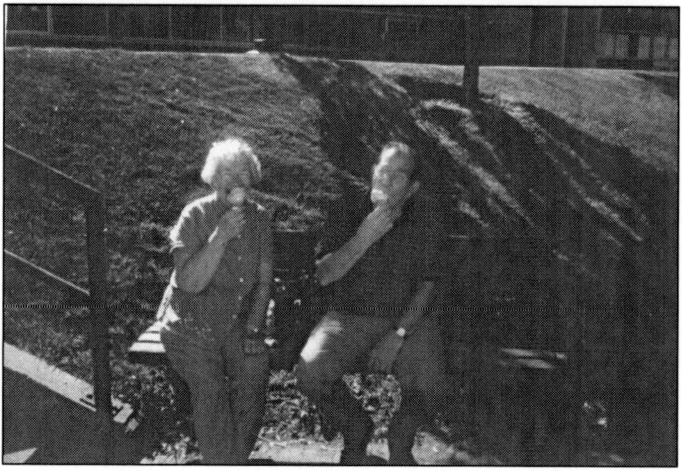

DAVID MOULDS

BD8 & BEYOND

DAVID MOULDS

BD 8 & BEYOND

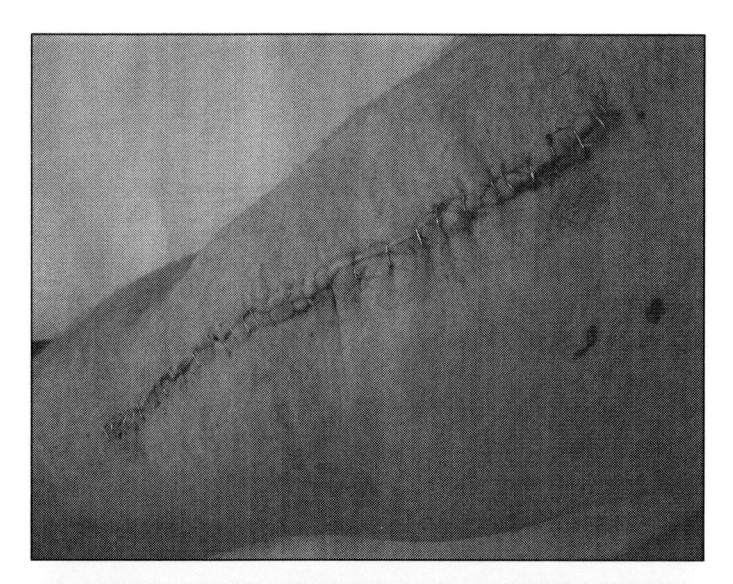

Chapter 11

Working in the Lift & Escalator business was ok but it didn't pay enough 'bread' and we were exploited in my opinion. The lads I worked with were mainly sound, Sam, Roger, AJ, Mal and Chris but I was applying for everything I could and in November I got a break, or so I thought.

I went to worked for a large bakery in Leeds on the maintenance, the money was better and the overtime was there to be had but the shift pattern was shite. 8 hour shifts meant you had to work six days a week which were on a rotation and actually meant, you never a full 24 hours off!! The work was non-stop and anyone that works, or has worked in the food industry knows that break downs mean big money losses straight away, so the maintenance lads had it right on their shoulders. Within a few month, I was Deputy Engineering Manager and managed to implement a 12 hours shift system, which meant the lads had a couple of days off each week, much to everyone's benefit.

Times were still very hard for us as a family with Lucy winning skating tournaments all over the place, Sue was spending all her time working or with Lucy's skating and I was either at the bakery or on the doors. It wasn't long before things had to give and we were stretched that far that our marriage once again hit the wall and we split for the second time. That old yarn about the seven year itch..........we split after seven years and then split again after a further seven years!!!!

I wasn't doing too badly financially; we had a few quid coming in from the doors and I was getting plenty of shifts in at the bakery. I had a couple of brief flings and then went steady with Karen, a girl from Heckmondwyke, we had a good laugh and I could let my hair down with her. We went over to Harrogate one weekend to see Doug, one of my mates from the scooter club days, great great friend of mine, even through to this day. Doug and I have our birthdays two days apart and even though we didn't see a great deal of each other, we always kept in touch. He would regularly fall out with a lot of our other mates when we were younger but it was different with he and myself and we always had q solid bond. We had a cracking weekend, a total chill from the 'rat race' and he was made up for me, that I was spending time with someone new and was in a happy state of mind. I acted like I was 21 again for three months and then went back to wife Sue and daughter Lucy to try make things work. Our relationship was never even remotely the same but with Lucy's skating career, it was more a convenience I think.

The Ice Skating was costing £1,000 a month, with the training fees, travel and all the extra's. Sue and I had two separate lives really and it was hard going but to see your child succeed in a really difficult and competitive sporting environment is a brilliant feeling. I managed to acquire a phone number for the National Lottery and rang them regarding sport funding. The guy I spoke to was really off hand with me and wanted to know how I'd got the number and was adamant that there was no funding for the ice skating until an individual had reached international level. I questioned this and said that if the individual's parents couldn't afford to fund a kid with talent, then that talent would be wasted and lost for ever. He replied that that was how the 'system' worked, so whilst I was giving him a few choice words, he hung up! I was quite bemused because at that time, the public was led to believe that the National Lottery was funding sport in massive way, not so from where I was standing. So be it, no let up for my day job and the door jobs.

Back in the bakery, the shifts were hard and demanding, I was working in very varied heat conditions. The large blast freezers could go down as far as -40 degrees C and the large fryer, up to 300 degrees C and one was called to hundreds of pieces of machinery per shift. The food industry calls for non stop maintenance because the cooking, baking or frying of produce doesn't come to a halt when a breakdown occurs, so quick repairs are imperative so as not to lose up to thousands of pounds worth of production.

I worked with some good engineers at that time, as well as some complete arseholes!!! A guy called Simon Greenwood was set on and worked on the same shifts as myself, we worked together and became good mates, although he did say that he waiting to start as an engineer at Fields printers in Bradford. I'd applied at Fields a few times myself but to no avail, you had to be related, or know someone who worked there to have a chance of a start. Eddie Caffrey was the electrical deputy engineering manager and between us we were trusted to interview candidates for vacant engineering positions. Eddie was a top bloke and really new his stuff and later would get to be Group Engineering Manager.

I was constantly at loggerheads with a lot of staff at the bakery over various issues, they seemed to be set in their ways and it was difficult to progress with the maintenance side of the business at times. A lot of staff were on minimum wage and a few weren't the brightest buttons on the coat, although, at the other end of the scale, there were some highly skilled and very clever staff that worked there. The place was constantly edging on with expansion and was owned and run by the Wood family. David was the Managing Director and was approximately 30 years old, he ran the day to day 'wheels' of the place, with a few managers underneath him. He was a very clever bloke with some good ideas for the future but never listened to anyone else's point of view and was a total pain to get on with most of the time. Working life could be an absolute nightmare at that place if you weren't thick skinned, one of David's managers was a guy called Wormley and let's just say that he and I didn't really see eye to eye most of the time. He seemed to think that he was the be all and end all and I had to do my upmost to stop myself from knocking all his teeth out of his fucking head!! Even so, I, did express my opinions to him on more than one occasion. We were on 'walkie talkie' radio system and after having a lengthy exchange of words over a couple of breakdown jobs, I told him and another manager to get into the yard so we could sort out the problem face to face, so to speak. That only ended with me being reprimanded and in a management 'bollocking' meeting that lasted an hour and a half.

Over in 'Clecky' things had got a little bit naughty and after a couple of visits from Bradford City's Ointment boys, things came to a head. It kicked off in the foyer and spilled out onto the forecourt. Gary was in the thick of it and got glassed in the chest and the chin before 'Scrap' pulled him free with the aid of a couple of tins of gas. After getting stitched up at the Infirmary Gary rang me and said that confrontations with the City boys were fairly even and we were leaving it there....so that was that.

I had to put more effort into the doors after that because Gary, Slick and Tony were arrested on drugs charges. Gary also had possession of a firearm, CS gas, coshes and knuckle dusters, so things didn't look too good. All three were banged up in Armley nick at Leeds on remand, while the lawmen put their case together.

The lads down in Cleckheaton were solid, backed me up and worked well for me. Danny, Martin, Steve, Gary, Bri Pollard, Lee, Big Tony (the black guy, that was shot in Bradford, years earlier) all knew most of the locals and the gaffers in the three manors that we had were easy to get on with. I took Gary's girlfriend, Lindsey, to Armley a fair few times to see him and was always in high spirits and hopeful that he'd soon be out.

One of the few days I had off from the bakery over the Christmas period was New Years Day and there was an event on at A.J's club in Bradford that needed a couple of guys on the door in the afternoon. It was a sixth form Christmas bash, so I knew that they'd all be arseholed and carry on but what the hell, work was work. Geoff and I arrived and the place was heaving with 16, 17 and 18 year olds, all letting their hair down, now they'd escaped the 'reigns' of a family Christmas. There were quite a few Teachers there to keep them in check but it was comical watching them really, as they didn't stand a chance! Our job was mainly to make sure that there was no real trouble and to stop any undesirables entering the 'do'. One of the organisers told us that there was a possibility a couple of Asian lads that had been expelled might turn up. The 'do' was going fine, apart from one or two revellers that had to dealt with for carry on after having a few too many 'gargles' and then the Asian lads turned up. There were six of them and the 'mouth piece' at the front was giving it large threatening us with all kinds if we didn't let him in. A couple of teachers identified the lads that had been expelled and said that the others weren't legible to be there either. They'd managed to get into the foyer but we had the entrance covered and told them the score, to which they replied that we were going to be cut up. We tried to defuse the situation and talk them off but as soon as the front guy put his hand inside his coat, whilst telling me I was a dead man, it was game over. I rushed straight into them, with Geoff backing up and we bashed a couple of them as we bundled them through the doors and down the steps. No weapons were on show, so we think they were just 'fronting' it but they rushed the door twice and after coming off worse both times, left but not before saying they'd be back to sort us. This was mainly an Asian area so we were expecting a bit of a back lash and one of the teachers called the law. Sure enough, shortly after, a few motors turned up and a dozen or so lads were on show with a few tools but before it turned nasty, the Police sirens were heard and that was the end of it. The 'do' ended nicely and Geoff and myself nipped off for a beer or two.

I teamed up with John Celebanski, the boxer and landlord I mentioned earlier. I was hoping that with John's contacts in the pub game and the boxing, I'd be able to pick up a couple of decent venues and lads to man them. I'd worked at a few boxing/dinner functions that were organised by John, in Bradford town centre and all had gone well, so I thought I was on a winner.

Back at the bakery, things were moving forward, extra land, adjacent to the main site had been purchased and building work had started. My mate Simon had left and got the maintenance job at Fields, the printing place in Bradford and Eddie had progressed to drawing up all the plans for the new build. I was taking on more responsibility with the shift lads but was still 'hands on' and towing the line, with the odd fall out along the way.

I managed to book a few days off and headed for Great Harwood, Blackburn, Lancashire. Sean was getting wed to Karen and the venue for the stag 'do' was Ostend, Belgium. There was a total of thirteen of us sat on a train early doors on the Friday morning, heading for London, where we were to exchange trains down to Dover and then on the ferry across to Ostend. I'd met a few of Sean's mates before, so I wasn't totally 'on my own' so to speak. Billy, Zoy, Dickey, Spud, myself, Sean and the rest, a good set of boys really and it was going to be a good weekend. Early doors in Trafalger Square and the place was as packed as ever, both with punters and pidgeons! A small shop across the way was lucky enough to have our custom....or rather not. I think that I was probably the only one to pay for anything but the poor owner was well down on stock by the time we all departed! Not good and definitely not clever! We were having a steady drink as we lazed on the train on the way down to Dover, with one or two of the guys catching a bit of 'shut' eye for good measure. We were lucky enough to be booked on one of those new Hoverspeed ferries so our travel time was cut to half and all were buzzing.

We reached our digs and got checked in, a couple of the guys were straight into the tidy landlady of the small hotel, with fancy chat up lines, which was a giggle and she gave as good as she got! We had a decent day on the 'lush' and got to know where most of the sights were, one or two obviously hit the 'red light' section and, as always on these kind of weekends, it's never mentioned again.

Saturday is football day almost all over the world and was stated before hand that we all had to where 'colours', so you can imagine to boos, cheers and jeers, when I rocked up in a 'mighty' Leeds shirt. Apart from my good self, there were a mix of Blackburn, Burnley and England tops on show, so after a hearty breakfast, we were heading for the boozers. We met up with 'stag' do from the Midlands and they were a mix of Villa fans and Wolves lads. We had a few games of pool for quids and there was quite a bit of banter regarding teams and where we all came from, before we left and headed further into the town. Down the steps and into a big Karaoke bar, which seemed to go on forever!! There were pool tables, an arcade, food tables, T.V's, the lot really. The bar was oval and in the middle of the room, with three blokes serving on, all our guys went to one side, so I nipped round the other, consequently getting served first. I was feeling rather pleased with myself until I turned round and saw around thirty Chelsea fans, all eyeballing me!! I f I'd been 'crewed' up, there wouldn't have been any conversation but because I was on my 'Jacksey', a few of those Blues, some in colours, some in suits, sauntered over and stated chatting. Leeds had done them at home 3-1 a couple of months since, so I was having a bit of a giggle and a laugh with these guys, with them buying me a couple of beers for my cheek. It could have turned nasty though when Sean's mate Spuddy started shouting over to me, asking why I was drinking 'with those Cockney cunts'!!! one or two of the younger Chelsea lads were wanting a pop but the older end and myself, luckily calmed it down. That fucking Spuddy just laughed, ha, barmpot Burnley boy! I ended up standing on the table and singing Baker Street on the Karaoke to them, which went down quite well. They bid us fair well and did one, just before the Midlands boys turned up. Leeds had just lost in the quarter finals of the F.A cup against Wolves (that scruffy looking fucker Goodman, did the damage!) and one of the Midlands lads decided he'd had enough ale to start trying to take the urine out of me. He was spouting about Goodman and how shite Leeds were etc, the usual claptrap. I played it down but inside, I really wanted to knock all the shit out of this wanker but also, I didn't want to be the one who ruined the weekend. One or two of the Midland lads were sound and things were nipped in the bud. Sean and myself told the lads that we were moving to the next bar and we'd see them in there, so as I left, I gestured to a couple of the Midland boys that I was leaving. The next instant, I was kicked from behind, right under the armpit but I managed to keep my feet and spun round to see one of the Wolves fans stood there shouting that I was a smug cunt. I think he was a bit shocked that I hadn't gone over and when I fronted him and moved toward the twat, he backed off and apologised, saying he thought I was being funny with them!!?? I threatened to knock the fucker out but Sean pulled me away and we left it at that.

That evening, we again met up with half a dozen of the Midlands guys and the 'cowardly' kicker was with them. He apologised for the earlier incident and we just got on with having a good old night on the tiles. One or two of the guys sought out some of the local 'hookers', which is fair enough and it's a well known fact that whatever happens on a weekend away, stays away.

At the end of the night, there were a few of us in the bar at our hotel and there were still, four of the Midlands lads making up the numbers. Our boys drifted off to bed and there I was, left with our 'Black Country' friends. Two of them were bollocks and staggered out and then one fell off the stool, struggling to get back up. I looked at the 'kicker' and said "that's that then, you'd best put your mate to bed". He eyeballed me for a couple of seconds and then picked his buddy up, said his farewells and buggered off.....weird twat! A top weekend overall and a great set of blokes to spend it with........home, with a thick head for a day or two!

Steve, the gaffer at the Rio club had sold up to Paul Sewell who was the D.J, known to those in the 'trade' as Ziggy for some strange reason. He was in some kind of partnership with Steve for a while before doing the deal. Paul and myself had crossed swords a few times in the past and although I tried my best to get on with him, he had this real condescending tone about him which really got under your skin at times. He was constantly being smart with me and talking about being offered different door contracts, he also tried to 'hijack' my regular doormen that worked on the Rio door by telling them that if they worked for him direct, they would have a bit more money. I got wind of this through Bob and some of the lads denied knowledge of it when confronted but

I did tell them that I know that Paul had another crew in mind that if they went to work for him, it wouldn't be for long. In the end, I lost my rag with his two faced attitude, told him to pay me the balance and sort his own fucking door out. Although he struggled for that weekend, he eventually got sorted with his new crew of boys and that was that. I did contemplate 'smartening' the prat but knew he'd fuck up and get his comeuppance at some point. With everything he did or said, Paul was just one of those blokes that always had you wondering if he had ulterior motives and more often than not….he did!

Kinder was released from Armley after 12 months or so on remand after the court case fell down due to lack of evidence, although Slick got five year. There was a bit of a rumour spilling around that Gary had done some sort of deal but that was a load of shite and a couple of arseholes got smartened up in the process of that little story being put to bed. He married Lindsey and decided to pack the door side of things in altogether, so there I was, best man for a fourth time………that job was still as daunting as ever and didn't get any easier!

Tom, along with his son Derrick, the Glaswegian blokes who owned Foxy's in Cleckheaton, sold up and took on the Five Flags at Denholme. Wetherspoons took over and revamped Foxy's, they brought there own crew of boys in and I couldn't get a foot hold at all. Richard 'the Bulldog' worked the door at the Flags, along with Stevie Spalding and one or two others on rotation but it only lasted a year or so, as Tom was ill and sold up to move away….God bless you Tom…a really nice guy.

The Five Flags wasn't too far away from the Rock n Heifer, where we'd done a fair bit of work. All around that area, there seemed to be plenty of 'boys' that weren't averse to mixing it with the door staff. We'd had a couple of heavy incidents at the Rock, the main one was one New Year when Myself, big John and Geoff were at it in the doorway with the Thornton lads. There were iron bars, bricks, table legs..... pretty much the works apart from shooters. We came out of it ok but there was plenty injured and claret all over the bloody foyer area. The gaffer wasn't too pleased, although we managed to get through the rest of the night incident free.

Although big John Celebanski was a nice bloke, we weren't exactly hitting it off as partners and raking in the dosh, venues were hard to come by and so were good, licensed doormen. John and I called it a draw and I managed to get on board with Kevin Spratt, an ex-pro boxer who had a lot of doors in Leeds but needed a few guys to help out on his Bradford doors. This turned out to be really hard graft because all the venues Kev had required licensed boys and they all had to be on the books and paying tax etc.....I was struggling to get the guys to work for less 'wedge' than they were used to.

Chapter 12

At the bakery, the majority of machinery that was bought was all second hand. Certain pieces of kit were decent and some were just rubbish and hardly any of it worked when we acquired it but the gaffer was adamant that it was all good stuff and the engineers were told to bring them up to scratch. I took on the job of refurbishing some of the 'would be' scrapped off machines and bringing them back to life. The new site was half way to being finished, so I set up 'shop' in the new building with my broken, crippled machines. I had a radio on full belt, all the tools I needed and very little interruptions….great. I was well into the job, decent hours, enjoying all aspects of the refurbishments and still had some input into the running of the maintenance team. All was about to change though and for the better I might add!

Simon rang me up from Fields printers and said that there was an opening for an engineer and I had to ring the engineering manager, who at the time was a guy called Richard Warnick After a couple of interviews, I got a start date for April 1999.

There was a re-structuring of the engineering department going on at that time, so myself, Simon and Pete Kirrane, (Pete started the same day as I had), were putting in a hell of a lot of overtime hours. The money was good but the work was quite demanding, although the pressure wasn't as 'heavy' as it had been in the food industry.

The printing industry is pretty 'clicky' and these printers had more perks than you could shake a stick at! Even the warehouse and packing teams had plenty of 'extra's', in fact everyone except the Engineers had a piece of the cake. Without the Engineers, the place would have come to a standstill but there was no way we could negotiate the same shift rates or call-out pay as the rest of the workforce. The Engineers, Printers, Warehouse staff, 'Make ready', Packing staff etc are all pieces of the jigsaw and all play a part in the manufacture of the end product, therefore everyone should be treated with the same respect. In most industries it seems to be the case that the Maintenance Engineers are looked upon as a necessary evil and not as major players in the 'make up' of a successful company. Anyhow, the money was there to be earned and the conditions were good so………crack on!

It was at that time on one of my shifts, that I met up with Mick Robbo, one of the printers. As I mentioned previously, I'd had a run in or two with him and a few other guys from the Clayton area a number of years back. We had a laugh reliving an altercation or two and have been good mates ever since.

I went on a course to the Bobst factory in Lausanne, Switzerland to get 'clued up' on the Registron Systems that were instrumental in the running of the printing press's at Field Packaging. The course was for one week and I went with Pete, who I was to be partnering on our shift system. We were sat in the departure lounge at Leeds/Bradford airport deciding who was going to look after the expenses money, when we suddenly realised that the tickets were actually Business Class!! Into the 1st class lounge, feet up and chilling without all the 'hustle and bustle' of the 'run of the mill' departure lounge.

The hotel was ok and was situated on the edge of Lake Geneva, which was very picturesque. The Bobst factory was a few miles away and we were picked up the next morning and driven to the site before being given a guided tour. This was a large site and full printing machines along with a host of accessories. The factory is out in the 'sticks' and there are even petrol pumps that are subsidised for the staff!

We found a great little boozer round the corner from the hotel called the White Horse and this was to be the closest to an English drinking venue that we came across. There was a 'Happy Hour' each evening and the time of this was advertised outside the place at lunchtime. So after having a decent chat with the little blonde barmaid, we were able to find out the 'Happy Hour' time for each day the evening before! Quality….we were able to use the 'two for one' drinking offer to its maximum. Hence to say, we weren't always in the best condition when being picked up at 6.30 the morning after. All in all, this was a good trip and was to stand us in good stead with the work we were doing at Fields.

The British Ice Skating Championships were held in Belfast that year and I went and stayed in a large boarding house in the Newtownards Road, with Sue, Lucy and a few others from Lucy's training set up. England were playing Scotland in first leg of the play-offs for the European Championships. I asked the owner of the digs which would be the best boozer to grace with my presence to watch the match and was told in no uncertain terms that it would be a very bad move for me to go boozing in any of the pubs in the area! Fair enough then,

I took the blokes advice and watch England do the 'Jocks' 2-0, on the T.V. in the digs. Lucy had a decent championship but alas, wasn't up in the top three skaters.

The Millennium New Year was painted up as major event when all the computers, databases, TV's etc, were all going to go tits up and screw up the whole world. Well that didn't happen and on Old Years Night, we had a big family gathering at Phil and Mary's, place (my wife's sister). A decent night with Karaoke, food, drink and fireworks, great until her half brother Chris, decided to push me over the edge. Two things that are really annoying and not up for discussion, are, being called a full weight wanker....with meaning and being prodded in the chest whilst being lectured. Chris had a problem at the time with some guys over money and drugs and after I showed some concern, he proceeded to tell me I was out of my depth with his finger banging into my chest. When he picked himself up, he carried on with his verbal abuse and prodding, telling me that I was a complete wanker, so he very quickly found himself sat on his shitter again. His verbal tirade came to an abrupt end and I told him to deal with his problems on his own. I was disappointed with myself for bashing him but felt he didn't really leave me much of a choice at the time. Most of the family, I think, agreed and I did receive an apology from Chris shortly after. We are to this day fine and I occasionally see Chris and we have a chat.

The Craven Heifer at Manchester Road in Bradford was under new management, opening as Mr Q's and I was supplying the doorman through a contract with Kev Spratt. On the opening night, I worked on the door with Bob Siree and although the night went reasonably well, this was an 'open' venue that really needed three guys to man it properly. I got a couple of decent blokes from the other side of Leeds to work the place and I was damn lucky because these guys were good doormen and the only reason I'd got them at the low rate we were paying, was because there was no work in their area. Bradford City's Ointment boys began hanging out in the boozer and from time to time, this proved a slight problem. A couple of times the landlord rang me to say there was some grief, the lads weren't too pleased with him, under minding them! One Saturday evening after a game I went down and it had kicked off, the three of us were up against a dozen pissed up footie fans in the middle of the busy pub. Pool cues, pool balls, glasses and chairs were flying everywhere as 'normal' punters ran for cover. We got the upper hand after three or four of their lads had gone down and a couple of local lads had assisted us. It settled down after that confrontation and there wasn't another major incident with those lads. I was also supplying Scully's bar with door staff at that time. This was a place in Heckmondwyke and anybody that is familiar with the area will know that it can get a bit tasty from time to time. I went through quite a few different guys in a short space of time before Martin and Steve worked it on a regular basis. These two had done plenty of work for myself and Gary, down in Cleckheaton and were an 'ok' pair of lads. They had a bit of a set too with a rugby team in a 'curry' gaff in Cleck and although the odds were massively against them, they came out on top, damaging quite a few of the opposition. They were promptly arrested and slapped with a Community Service Order.

We were still getting to plenty of Leeds games and the boys were 'living the dream' under manager David

O'Leary. We went to Rome to play AS Roma in the UEFA Cup in the 4th round in March 2000. Our group of 4 flew out from Stansted Airport and in the group was myself, Hayton, Trevor, and a guy called Chaddy. Chaddy was once working away in Gambia, (or the like) and after getting a cab from the hotel, was kidnapped, driven into the wild and held at gunpoint. A few Gorilla types turned up and after a load of shouting, it was apparent that he wasn't the chap that they wanted, so they just left him there! The local law said that it was a miracle that they didn't shoot him dead! Anyhow, we had a train journey into Rome and on our arrival, flagged down a cab. The cheeky bastard took us in a big circle to the hotel, which was actually a 'shit and a piss' form the train station! We were running quite late, so, checked in and got a cab to the ground. The cabbie wouldn't take us up the main road to the ground, he said it was dangerous, so we were on our toes. There was quite a bit of 'fisty cuffs' outside the ground and a few casualties running around with 'claret' leaking from their wounds, all part and parcel really. We were caught up the middle of large groups of Leeds lads running at the Roma boys and visa versa, this was quite a volatile atmosphere.

It was a typical atmosphere with English fans getting showered with objects from the home fans but the game was ok and Leeds held their own. Just before half time I noticed that the local 'Plod' were pulling their face scarves up and drawing their batons! We moved into the middle of our section and I told a mate of mine, Gary Kilmartin, who was there with his young lad Josh, to do the same. Shortly after, the law waded into blokes, women and kids, hitting anyone with those damn batons, for no reason at all...bastards!

The game ended in a 0-0 draw and the fun was about to begin. Outside the ground were lines of armed police, who's only concern was to get the Leeds fans onto the buses, which were going either to the town centre or the airport. If you argued, you got battered and thrown on the nearest bus! I was with Hayton and we'd lost Trev and Roger. Apparently Trevor managed to get off the airport bus after been whacked by a lawman and knocked about. This was his first ever match and he had no idea that this kind of thing went on, he was pretty put out!! Ha ha. After jumping from the bus in the centre, Paul and I were a fair trek from our hotel and set off walking, only to find that The Ultra's, Roma's firm, were patrolling the streets in cars as well as on foot. These arseholes have a bad reputation but very rarely stand toe to toe with other mobs (as Man U proved more recently), they pick groups off and use ambush methods. We were struggling to dodge the large groups that were tooled up on the streets and almost got run down by a couple of motors. We ended up 'legging' it into a restaurant and having some feed until the situation eased off.

Next day we walked round Rome, admiring the sights and stopping off for beers at numerous boozers. We met up with a few mates from Bradford, Chris, Timmy, Royston and Phil Mac and together we had a damn good session on the ale! Paul and myself also took in a few sights, incorporating the Coliseum and the Vatican. That evening we came across a bar on a main street that looked half decent and headed passed the doormen and down the steps inside. We got beers and I looked around the drum, only to find that there was only one way in and out. It was a long cellar bar with three or four rooms and I noticed we were getting eye-balled and surrounded by a couple of dozen local faces. This was a naughty gaff and after a few choice words, we quickly hit the exit before the shit hit the fan. We found another bar and to our surprise, the great John Charles was present with a small group of his friends. We got chatting, shared drinks and were having a decent time when half a dozen Leeds lads came in. these young arseholes started slating the Leeds legend and myself and Paul fronted them up before fucking them off outside onto the cobbles. All in all, a good away trip and a decent result.

A month later Leeds played Galatasaray in Turkey in the first leg of the semi finals and it was a game that I'm glad I didn't attend. Numerous Leeds lads were ambushed and stabbed in various locations in and around Istanbul and two of these were Kevin Speight and Chris Loftus, who were tragically murdered. Ironically, the game went ahead and naturally, with the two deaths overshadowing everything else, Leeds lost the game 2-0. Now if the deaths had been caused by an English club's fans, there is no doubt whatsoever that all English clubs would have been banned from European competitions, as was the case after the Hysel Stadium incident. Many teams have been involved in serious violent scenes at games involving Turkish teams, Man Utd, Leeds, Arsenal and Panathanaikos to name a few. There are also plenty of stabbings and the odd shooting at the derby games involving Galatasaray and Fenerbahce. On arrival in Turkey, opposing fans are welcomed with banners stating; "welcome to hell" and "Die", amongst others. Very little action is taken against the Turks, or any other country really regarding football violence, yet the English are punished severely at the drop of a hat....why the fuck is that then!!??

Leeds drew the second leg at Elland Road 2-2 two weeks later and went out of the cup under a very volatile atmosphere, with Galatasaray fans being stopped from attending the game for their own safety.

November that year and we were on our way to Milan in the Champion's League. We'd beaten them at Elland Road a couple of months earlier but needed a result in the famous San Siro stadium to progress in the competition. No English club had ever won there and nobody really gave us a prayer in hell.

We'd travelled from Stansted airport to Venice and then up to Milan on the train. We were six strong in our party, Pollard, Hayton, Mal, Chad, Trevor and myself. This was only Trevor's second football game and after the incidents in Rome, I didn't think he'd be 'batting' again but fair play to him.

The train journey up to Milan was a few hours long and the attendants weren't up to supplying us with very much alcohol, so we made do with some 'blow' that was kindly brought along by one of the lads. We were all giddy as fuck when we reached the hotel and went straight on the lash. There were a group of Blackburn Whites in the hotel bar and as usual in these situations; there was a loud mouth twat making a pillock of himself and slating the barman off. After an hour or so of 'bad mouthing', the lad said he was shutting the bar and after slinging the loud mouth prat out, I persuaded the barman to keep the bar open for us……..he was quite amused that we'd christened him 'Frank'! we went on to get quite hammered that night and to Pollards amusement, I even made a 'barfing' deposit in the flowerbeds!! (I personally put it down to too much 'blow')!!

Next day after a solid breakfast, w were looking forward to a good day on the beer and hopefully getting a result against Milan. Unfortunately, a couple of Leeds fans had been stabbed, one in the stomach with a broken bottle, so the lawmen, in there wisdom, had decided to close all the bars in Milan!! Now, imagine 7,000 Leeds fans wandering around the centre of Milan, all looking for a bar that was willing to serve them and constantly being refused. The atmosphere just got more and more tense until it ended up with violent confrontations with the law.

Our group were lucky enough to find a licensed side street café that was owned by an Inter Milan fan and he was more than happy to welcome us in with open arms. All our phones were constantly ringing, as fans all over Milan were looking to find a gaff where they could get a drink but if we'd disclosed our location, we'd have been swamped. We spent around six hours in the bar/café and as well as having a bite to eat, we drank every drop of alcohol that the guy had on the premises.

The journey to the San Siro was manic!! The tube trains were packed with an army of Leeds fans and the excitement of the walk up to the ground was highlighted when the stadium came into view. The Italian lawmen didn't give a monkey's arse about the fan's safety and proceeded to filter all the Leeds lads into the nearest entrances as quickly as possible. Behind the goal at the 'Leeds' end was absolutely packed as thousands of fans were crammed into the same area! It became really dangerous with fans almost being crushed under the constant stream of bodies and eventually it kicked off. There were battles with the law and the 'Whites' even turned on each other to save being crushed as the surge through the turnstiles continued.

I'd had a small op a few days previous and had half a dozen stitches in my groin, which wasn't really the best preparation for a game of this stature but what the hell! As the melee continued, I ended up in between the seats a few rows further down than when I had started and knew that the wound in my groin was bleeding! Just my fucking luck! The law seemed to have calmed things down slightly but through the gaps on the terrace, I could see an old mate of mine, Nicky Muff, throwing punches for all he was worth at anyone in striking distance, ha, damn barmpot!

Milan missed a penalty before Matteo put Leeds in front, which had Leeds fans in Heaven and had every A.C fan snivelling in their soup. Hee hee. The game ended in a 1-1 draw, which put Leeds into the last 16. Milan fans were nowhere to be seen when we came out of the ground and we went the 'lush', having a serious drink to celebrate!

The next morning I visited a chemist, with Pollard in tow, to try and purchase some dressings for the groin wound, there was quite a spill of blood that had leaked from the split stitches. We were struggling in the chemist, as neither the bloke nor the woman could speak our lingo and in the end, I just dropped my strides and pointed to the bleeding wound!! Pollard was on the floor howling with laughter but it did the trick and I got a pile of dressings and anaesthetic cream.

On the train back to Venice we misheard the announcement and got off at Vicenza. We had to jump on the next train and although all worked out ok, we nearly missed the sodding flight. So home we went, with the Christmas break looming on the horizon.

Chapter 13

It was a few days before Christmas and after breaking up from work, foremost on everyone's mind was going out on the beer and partying. Bradford had always had some great pubs and a good night life but in recent years a lot of the pubs had been replaced by crappy wine bars that were full of young trendy tossers and student types and most of the 'town boys' seemed to have disappeared.

We were on a mission to let our hair down and have a top day on the booze. A few back street pubs with a few old mates and we were on our way into town to meet up with all the guys from work. We entered the Queens after a good gallon and we were buzzing. It was busy with Christmas 'finishers', spirits were high and the atmosphere was tripping. There were five of us in our direct group and the other four mingled with all our workmates while I had a chat with one of the doormen, who I'd known for a number of years. After a couple of drinks, everyone started to move to the next pub, I was with my mate Si and after bidding John, the bouncer, farewell, we went to catch up with the crowd. As we approached the next bar, there was a little bit of a queue and as we got to the door, Si started to enter but one of the two Asian doormen said I'd had too much to drink and couldn't come in. I tried to explain that I hadn't and had a dodgy knee but they were so arrogant and full of themselves and were having none of it. A couple of mates came out and after a short conversation, common sense prevailed and we persuaded the two 'jobsworths' to let me in. Less than half an hour later and it was time to move on but on the way out, one of the doorman thought he'd make a few smart 'quips' and have a laugh on our behalf. Well, words were exchanged and the smaller of the two doormen took a cheap shot and punched me on the back of my head, as I turned, the cheeky 'tool' digged me straight in the middle of the cheek. Well all hell broke loose and the two fellas had to earn their pay, or, rather not! I managed to land a decent shot on my assailant and sent him flying backwards, his partner, who was a lot taller and a bit of a boxer, so I learned later, came forward and although I was stood a step lower down, I caught him with an uppercut that went straight through his guard and he ended up with an open wound from his eye to his hairline. These two had opened a hornet's nest and got well stung as three or four, pissed off guys got weighed into them. They were very good with the verbal but after having the shit knocked out of them in the foyer, they ended up running into the bar, crying for help and covered in 'claret'. Start it………. finish it.

Unfortunately for me, it hadn't crossed my mind that the two so called 'doormen' would get the law and start searching all the pubs in the surrounding area but hey ho, that's exactly what these two clowns did and inside the hour, both Si and myself were sat in the cold cells for the rest of the night…………………..

We were arrested as we left a bar in the middle of Bradford and the law weren't exactly light gloved about it. The Bobbies quizzed and chased, wanting to know who else was involved in the incident at The Bank pub and when no other names came forward, they said that Simon and myself would carry the whole load. The doormen said that I used a bottle, causing one of them to have the top of his head glued and that I had called them 'Black Bastards'. A right load of bollocks on both counts but the lawmen were going to nail me, no matter what. Now, these two 'doormen' said I'd gone off on one and attacked them with the back up of a couple of mates after arguing with them on the steps. Now then, there were no cameras, no bottle, no witnesses on the prosecutions behalf and the doormen even said that I didn't even go inside the pub!! Not a lot to work with but the CPS were adamant to go ahead and put a case against us. My brief said there was no way that it would get to court as they had nothing...........how wrong.

Back at work, I seemed to receive the full backing of the management and the General Manager, told me to keep him, personally, up to speed with the progress of all proceedings and he'd support me fully.

I didn't get to many footie games that year for obvious reasons, plenty of maintenance work, a reasonably low profile and numerous court appearances taking their toll.

Lucy had managed to earn a place on the Great Briton Skating Squad the previous year and had moved up to Aire so she could train at the Centrum Arena with most of the other squad members. Half a dozen of the skaters stayed in a large house with the coach, Joy. The cost was crippling but we were managing to sustain it.....just. Still travelling all over the UK for competitions, along with accommodation costs and constantly driving up to Aire and back, all added up. The biggest joke was the National Lottery's input. Lucy was entitled to funding after making National squad and we were sent a cheque for £200 for the year from The Sports Aid Foundation, which was laughable, as this covered less than one weeks expenses.......I almost sent the cheque back telling them to stuff it! Although Lucy had been winning plenty of competitions, she was having more than her fair share of injuries and the fees for consultants and physio's were an extra 'bag of coal' to carry. Week after week she was having treatment for hip, thigh and back pains and even the hospital scans were inconclusive as to the cause of the problems. We were open to any suggestions that could point us in the right direction and our next port of call was a physiotherapist in Halifax who had treated some of the Halifax Blue Sox players. She straight away told me to stop Lucy skating and diagnosed major damage to the spine!! We had further scans that confirmed Lucy had three vertebrae that were badly worn and two that were cracked..............that was that, no more freestyle skating. She was offered a place in the British Squad as a dance, pairs skater but after a short 'test drive', decided against that option. So, skating career over, a potentially great skating talent lost and one devastated teenage daughter. It was back to school sixth form with the view of heading off to University.

Kirrane was to get married to Sally in August that year and had arranged a stag weekend in Newcastle for a large group of us. Some really good lads, Pete, Shaun, Craig, Peg, Merv, Scott, Matt Adams, just to name a few. We went Quad biking on the way there and there were a few crashes but the funniest thing was the starter shouted to go and Merv just sat there as the rest of the Quads set off! Merv is totally deaf!! The hotel was in Gateshead and we met up with my brother Pete near the bridge and headed into Newcastle, stopping off at quite a few boozers on the way. The shit hit the fan in a pub near the Quayside, Pete, big Shaun and Craig were at it but the bouncers came running from all the boozers in the area and we definitely had to do one! We all got split up and as I was on the phone to Shaun, I was knocked over by a taxi! One minute I was chatting to him and the next, I was rolling over the bonnet and hitting the floor. I was still talking to Shaun as I lay on the deck and the taxi driver was all I a panic asking if I was ok!

The next morning I had a large black bruise, covering the outside of my thigh and was limping slightly to say the least. A few beers at lunchtime at Scotch Corner and although I was feeling sore, I was in a more relaxed state! We'd had a decent trip and we were all slightly worse for wear. Poor Matt just 'barfed' all the way home…..not in a good state at all!

Simon wanted to press some charges against the law for 'knocking' him about on the night of the arrest but had been well advised to stay clear of that avenue, although we both thought he had pretty good cause! The charges against Simon were dropped by the CPS but I was charged with actual bodily harm and assault with a weapon, although they did drop the racist factor and the affray charge. It turned out that one of the doormen at the Bank pub had done some work for us at the Rio club, a few years previous. Although I hadn't recognised him, I remembered the name and also remember, after giving him numerous chances to prove himself, having to lay him off because he wasn't right cracking as a doorman!! Maybe this was why the guy was feeding the law a load of old shite and trying to have me nailed. There were one or two magistrate court hearings and things seemed to be coming on top a little. I was advised to drop all contact with any doorstaff and basically told that it would be in my favour to stay well clear of any involvement to the supply of security in any shape or form. If not, the prosecution would do their up most to use it against me. The case was to go to Crown Court but my Barrister was adamant that there was very little evidence and no witnesses so in his opinion, it was highly unlikely that I would be found guilty. This was turning out to be a shitty year........... the skating, this pile of crap on my toes and to cap it all, Leeds losing in the semis of the Champions League.

I kept clear of most of 'our' doors and I threw the towel in regarding all the bouncing work and gave most of our guys contact numbers for work elsewhere. It was December and we were starting a five day Crown Court trial, my legal team were still convinced that the CPS didn't really have enough to go on and wouldn't have pursued the case if the doormen hadn't been of Asian origin even though there was no question of the case being racist.. The prosecuting Barrister obviously didn't think she had enough to win the case because she asked if I would be willing to except a 'Breach of the peace' charge and a 'Drunk and Disorderly' charge. We agreed that I would accept the charges but the two doormen wanted me charged with assaults, so the trial went ahead.!!

Throughout the trial there were unexplained discrepancies but everything went against me. Certain Police officers were adamant that I made no phone calls form the station and calls made earlier that night, were also discarded. I had spoken to Kev Spratt on the phone, outside The Bank pub about the two doormen, (they were working for him) but the doormen denied the call was made. These calls were evidence and proved that certain people weren't telling the truth on the stand and couldn't be deemed credible under oath but my phone bill, proving that the calls were made, was not allowed to be shown as evidence!! We had a statement from Kev but my 'Brief' decided not to use it. The prosecution had no solid evidence whatsoever, they stated that I didn't actually enter the premises, although I had over a dozen witnesses to say otherwise and could have actually called on another dozen!. Two friends of mine, Mal, a Leading Fireman and Greggy, who has his own local business, stood on the stand and both said they had been with me inside the premises but were both deemed as liars by the court!! The prosecution had no weapon and no witnesses to back up anything they said. All that aside, on the Friday afternoon, the jury came back with a close split decision. The judge was called Macallum and didn't seem a bad sort really, he seemed to prompt the jury in my direction. He said that he wanted any verdict to be clear cut and asked them, in turn, if they could resume on Monday morning. Most of them came up with excursuses as to why they would not be able to attend on the Monday, some said they could not have time from work, one or two had kids to look after and a couple said they worked for themselves and could not afford the time off. I was thinking, "This is my life you people are playing with and I want justice, not what's easier for your personal life!!!" The judge even offered to get an application passed for a Saturday morning court but that went down like a lead balloon as well. They went out again to consider and within half an hour, they were back and the fuckers nailed me to the floor. This wasn't a verdict related to "Without reasonable doubt", this was a case of "Let's get it over, I want my tea"!! So, to all you twelve people that sat on the Jury bench of my trial, at Bradford Crown Court, two weeks prior to Christmas 2001, you all should be thoroughly ashamed of yourselves, there was no real evidence and you couldn't get yourselves out of there quick enough to carry on with your, no doubt, pretty mundane little lives!

Sentencing was scheduled in January, after assessments, so Christmas was a pretty dismal affair that year. On return to work, I was hauled before Boxall, who's attitude had done a, 'full about turn'. He made it clear that if I did some 'stir', I was out of a job and even a non-custodial might mean my dismissal. Now, I always believe that when a man gives his word or commits to something, then his word is his bond and shows how tall a man stands. Mr Boxall now had me down as a 'major criminal' and had no intention of backing me up.

The day of the sentence hearing and I headed for the Crown Court with my wife and daughter. I had packed a bag to take with me, as I was expecting a custodial sentence of around 18 month. My top mate Sean had shown up from Blackburn to give some moral support and an hour later we all breathed a sigh of relief as the judge gave me 240 hours community service and a whacking fine.

I arranged to work the 'order' hours on a Sunday and work off any other days as quickly as I could. At work on the maintenance, I was contracted to work to full weekends in every five but the 'court order' work caused a slight problem. I offset any extra overtime that I worked against the Sundays and had to justify myself to Boxall, who just became total 'smart' with regard to my proposal and would have had me on my knees in order to keep the job, if he thought he could have got away with it! How people's attitudes change!!

The first day I turned up to work the 'order' hours, there was a big black guy who was as loud as they come and kept pestering me, trying to find out what my crime had been. After a couple of hours of this clown chewing my lug off, I blurted out what I was there for and he shut the fuck up, thank the Lord. I was amazed at how dim some of these 'cons' were, they stole from places where we were working and got nicked, obviously!! There was one lad there who'd had a piece bitten out of each of his ears!! He looked a right sight and had obviously pissed some fucker off! He would constantly say, "Give your head a shake", which was a saying that I began to use on a regular basis and now half of Yorkshire use the statement. 'Flash', a mate of ours is always into my ribs to come up with a new 'catch phrase' or saying but nothing has reared its head as yet. We worked at a Greyhound rescue centre for a while, gardening, painting and a few other chors, which was quite good, therapeutic in fact but the stupid bastards robbed the place and let all the dogs out, some dying after attacking each other. You can't educate shite, some of these fucked up halfwits were seriously deranged!

I finished the community order inside five months, involving painting, gardening, postal work, collections, sand bag filling and sorting out meals for the old folk, which was pretty good going for a 240 hour sentence.

Chapter 14

I'd had a week or so authorised break in the middle of the Community Order to go on holiday. It was my wife Sue and Russ's 40th birthdays and 'top man' Russ had booked a cruise for the three of us and Marg, in the Caribbean. We flew to Barbados, boarded the ship and then visited St Lucia, Grenada, Margarita, Caracao and Aruba. Russ and myself decided to defy the advice of the ship's crew and visit the nearest town to the port on the island of Margarita. We should have realised it wasn't too friendly when we were told not to wear any watches, rings or any other form of jewellery. We got a cab and one of the port security, an absolutely huge black guy just shook his head, after asking if we were sure we wanted to head in that particular direction. A few miles down the road and the cab pulled up, he dropped us at the top of the main street, stating that he didn't want to drive the car into the centre!!?? There were guys walking around with machetes and a sort of 'tumbleweed' blowing about.........it was like a setting from a dodgy film!! We were the only white faces on this 'film set' and the town seemed to stop dead, so we quickly headed into the nearest bar and out of the searing heat. The bar was empty apart from a big geezer who was watching basketball on the TV, he briefly eyeballed us and mumbled something. We had a couple of cold cokes and 3 bottles of Bud each and then struggled for ten minutes or so trying to pay the girl behind the bar, until the big fella intervened. He could speak perfect English!! He charged us $5 and explained that the dollar was worth plenty there and the President was round the bend but had a good relationship with the US ! Barmy. He ordered us a cab and we quickly did one. There was plenty to do on the ship and we made the most of it but not in the same vein as the Americans, they seemed to be filling their faces at every opportunity. There was a night club on one of the upper decks and one night myself and Russ were knocking a few back, when I experienced one of the funniest occurrences in my life. The music to 'Footloose' started and there was a guy stood on the dance floor dressed all in white and looking like a fifty year old John McEnroe. Well, this guy started dancing about at lightening speed and proceeded to crash into a load of seats and going arse over tit!! A couple rushed to his aide and helped him up and he tried to resume his dance, only to fall down between the tables in a heap! He was then carried out and for the rest of the cruise, he was using a walking stick and each time I saw him, I just cried laughing. We bought cigars in Caracao, spices in Grenada and diamonds in Aruba and all in all, a top bollocks jolly hol.

Russ had said to me that he was expecting the two doormen from the bank to get their comeuppance, as I had a 'Black Book' etched to the inside of my head and that's the way I've always lived my life. Although he didn't believe me, I told him that I'd let it lie and leave them be..........

I went up to Newcastle to stay with my brother Pete for a 'World Cup' final party weekend, my youngest brother Bryan was at my mums at the time and he went up with me. Bryan had moved out to live in Dubai through work a few years earlier and hadn't seen me or Pete for a while so it was set for a decent weekend. We weren't disappointed, it was a quality time but like all things, it had a downside! I tripped and landed on the arm of the settee, banging my side. I knew straight away that I had down some damage and for a short time, I couldn't actually get my breath, I was on the deck and I panicked and grabbed a bottle of ale. A good mouthful and I was gasping for all I was worth. The pain was excruciating and as I felt my side, I knew that I had broken three ribs...... as the saying goes.... 'When you slip in the cow field, you get covered in shit'!!

Back at work, a couple of days later, I was working on a job in the warehouse and was stood on some step ladders. When the ladders wobbled, I reached out and grabbed hold of a pipe, unfortunately it was a pipe that Matt Adams had left there and it wasn't attached!! I fell 8 feet to the floor, twisting in the air, so as to land on my back and try to protect my busted ribs!! Ha, cheers Matt. I lay there for a few minutes while the pain subsided and hoped that I had no further injuries. Thank fuck nobody actually saw hit the concrete. I did go to the hospital at Halifax but they wouldn't even check my ribs, saying it was unlikely that they were broken and were probably just bruised!!! Shite service.

Later that year, my great friend Gordon passed away, God rest his soul. As I mentioned earlier, Gordon was diabetic and in that year his health had deteriorated. We'd spoke in some depth about the consequences of his death regarding his family and he'd told me that financially, his family would be ok. He'd told me that he didn't fear death and would be happy to die that year so his wife, Linda and children, Adam and Emma would benefit from the life insurance. These conversations had, once or twice, ended in tears. We'd sing song lyrics at each other and laugh when one of us couldn't remember the words of certain songs. He was a top sort and a very good friend of mine. He had the Queen song, 'These are the days of our lives' played at his funeral, very fitting really..........

"Those were the days of our lives,
The bad things in life were so few,
Those days are gone now but one thing's still true,
When I look and I find, I still love you."

See you on the other side Gordon Ashley.

November saw Leeds visit Sheffield United for a midweek League Cup game and we were well fired up for it. All our coaches were pulled over before entering the city the law there seem to really hate you with a passion! They make you late for the game and either 'knock' you about or nick you if you complain and kick off. There were plenty of lads from both clubs outside the ground but the law were in abundance and kept the confrontations to a minimum. We lost the game 2-1 and went out of the cup. I'd had a burger outside the ground with my mate Carl Allen and I spent most of the night throwing up!!! Knocked out of the cup and fucking poisoned......cheers, you Blade Bitches!

We played those Blades again that season, in the quarter final of the F.A. cup, in March and got turned over again, that time it was 1-0. gutted again. As before, we were pulled over by the law as we entered Sheffield and a couple of them were making 2-1 gestures at us from outside the coach, relating to the League Cup game……very professional of them. I was hoping the coach might knock a couple of them over !!?? Inside the ground, Leeds fans ripped up seats and launched them down onto the pitch. It looked like it could escalate into a bit of a riot but the law were in control and quelled the situation.

My left knee was wearing, there were very little ligaments left, the cartilage was non existent and the joint was 'bone on bone' and there was a mention of a full replacement sometime in the future. In the meantime, I had a ligament operation on my right ankle at Bradford Royal and was in cast for a while. I told the consultant, Mr Shanker, about the pain in my side and the rib incident from the year before and he sent me for x-ray straight away. Sure as eggs are eggs, he confirmed that 3 ribs had been bust and there was a calcium build up round them. I had treatment to break down the 'build', which hurt like shit, no thanks to the Halifax General!!

The next, more serious, bombshell in that turbulent year was the disclosure that my dad had been diagnosed with lung cancer, a statement that rips a whole in you, as if it were yourself that had been diagnosed.

We'd bought the house next door, so as well as working full shifts at the Print plant, I was slogging it in the house and trying to spend time with my father. I managed to get the odd game under my belt but Leeds had hit the wall financially and we were pretty much fucked we were heading for the drop but a win away at the Arsenal, which just about gave the title to 'Scum Trafford' and a home win against Villa, kept us up.

Sue's dad Alan, was hospitalised when his body, basically had worn itself out though years of hardened alcohol and smoking abuse. He had been a successful painter and decorator in his time but as time went by, the smoke and drink had taken over. We had always got on sound but now he was on his last lap and Sue was spending a lot of her time with him. Obviously our marriage was struggling as we both spent time living, what appeared to be two separate lives.

My dad said that he didn't want to go into a Macmillan or Marie Curie hospice and that if he was on his way out, he wanted to 'go' at home. The pressure was telling on my mum, it was hard for her but she was there for him and I was doing my best to be there for her. My sister Pam was also doing her bit but brother Bryan living in Dubai and brother Pete up in Newcastle meant the family was split in body, if not in mind.

On the 4th November, I went to see my dad in the evening. He was in bed and the conversation wasn't brilliant as he was tiring through speaking and kept drifting off. As I was leaving the room, he said, "I'll se you lad" and I had a feeling they would be his last words to me. He lost the fight for life a few hours later, in the early hours of the 5th November 2003. This was a massive loss to us all and no matter how much sympathy and well being people send your way, it still knocks the shit out you and leaves you with a sense of numbness. There was a great turn out at the funeral and my dad got a good send off. He loved Frank Sinatra and I had a little smile to myself as "Fly me to the moon" played out at the end of the service.

After a small family and friends gathering, I went for a few drinks with my two brothers and my sister's son,

James, down in Bingley, where my mother and sister Pam live. We had a few beers and 'chewed the fat', after which, we each expressed our feelings for one another and then headed home.

Back home, Sue was waiting for my return, with some news of her own. Due to the amount of time she had been spending with her sick father and I with mine, we had hardly spent any time together and were pretty much virtual strangers really. Anyhow, Sue said that she thought we'd reached the end of the road together and as she was putting all her efforts into being there for her dad, I wasn't in the equation. I was mentally and physically drained, it had been a long day and I agreed that if that was her wish, then I would throw the towel in. The timing could have been better but as time has moved on, it has proved to have been the right move.

I worked like hell on the house next door and within weeks, just before Christmas, Sue moved in, until we decided on how to separate our assets, this was to prove an interesting situation to say the least!!

On the Monday 22nd December, I'd gone with the lads to watch Leeds v Man City at their new ground, Eastlands. We drew the game one each and apart from one of our lads, big Ian, having a verbal set-too with a couple of stewards, there wasn't much on the confrontation front.

We were sinking a few beers after returning to the Bedford pub, when Sue rang me and said that her dad had died. Not that a death is very nice at any time but over the Christmas period, it can be more of a testing time for families.

Alan's funeral was on New Years Eve and after he had been put to rest, everyone decided to give him a solid send off and run it through to New Year's Day. Myself and Russ were in the Duke William pub seeing in the New Year when, much to our surprise the snow began falling quite heavily. Now getting a taxi on that night of the year is always a pain and although I didn't live too far away, I wasn't really in a fit state to be staggering about on the road in the snow in the early hours. Luckily, there were two youngish lads with a sledge across the road from the pub and with the help of a 'tenner', I managed to persuade them to pull me on to my house..........best ten spot I've ever spent!! God only knows why the hell the two lads were there at that time!

A couple of months later I had a slight altercation in the Prince of Orange at Shelf after singing a tune on the Karaoke. These two clowns were talking the piss, so I threatened to 'smarten' them both up and then, after a few choice words with big Phil, the landlord, I was told I was barred. Across the road at the Shoulder of Mutton, not fifteen minutes later, the silly old pillock barred me for abusive language. I was with Russ at the time and I wasn't loud, the bloke just had it in for me and was trying to look the part. A couple of days later and I was in the Queen Victoria at the far end of the village, sat having a few beers with Russ and a table full of women. There was a band on at the time and as I recall, they were quite droll. I asked the singer to spice it up a little and he basically told me to get fucked, just as I stood up and gave him a piece of my mind, the pub fell quite silent..........barred again!! I was running out of local ale houses to drink in and hadn't actually knocked anyone over.

It was around that time when Gary Kilmartin passed away through cancer. He didn't smoke, was reasonably fit, a good husband and dad and just a decent bloke really. The Lord works in mysterious ways and seems to take more good people away than bad.

In that year of 2004 and Sue and I filed for divorce. Sue was seeing a new fella and Russ moved in next door to me. He had broken up with Sue's sister Margaret and was seeing Jayne. All change eh.

We went away to Old Trafford in February and got a 1-1 draw. The shit hit the fan inside the ground before half time, when a 'Red' jumped onto the dividing seating and headed for the Leeds boys. He was quickly battered and Leeds went into them.......quality. The stewards were helpless but the lawmen managed to get amongst the brawling fans and segregation was restored. It kicked off again in the second half but not for very long. The shit had well and truly hit the fan at Leeds United and the club was skint and in freefall. We went to Bolton with three games to go and got arsed 4-1, a result that confirmed our relegation from the Premiership.

I had another operation, preformed by the same consultant as the year before, Mr Shanker. From my accident in 1982, my left foot toes were 'clawed' and causing me some grief, so the toes were broken, the tendons altered and the toes 'pinned' and the foot and ankle cast in plaster.

On FA Cup Final day, I'd been down to the Brown Cow pub at Wyke with Roger, Hayton and a few other guys. We ran the 64 club, a sort of savings account for Cup Final day. Roger was and still is the main man running that and it makes for a top day out. Although I was on crutches, we'd had a good drink and a decent day but it didn't end there. I ended up in the Duke William boozer at Shelf and met up with Coleen and even though she was some years younger than myself, we got on great and were soon seeing plenty of each other. Col was a breath of fresh air to me, we had lots in common and even with the big age gap, we were good together, although we did have our moments..... after a bit of a tiff one night, I came home to find well over a dozen flower tubs from my front garden, emptied from boot to bonnet on my car... a women's wrath eh!!?? Shortly after, we had a top weekend away in Whitby and Robin Hood's Bay and on the way back I drove through a flock of sparrows that were on the road without slowing up. Coleen was 'to take away', she reckoned I must have flattened a few of them and didn't speak for the rest of the way home. Next day I told her that I had rang the RSPB and they'd confirmed that there were no fatalities!! Ha. I thought that was hilarious but when she found out I was taking the piss, it went down like a lead balloon.

I'd gone back to work with the cast still on and was keeping myself occupied with plenty of office work, although it was frowned upon by some of the management, who thought I should have stayed away. Sometimes, it's easier to take the piss and milk the situation!! I had the pins pulled out of the toes, which was an ordeal in itself and a large screw was left in the big toe as a 'stabiliser'.

My left knee was worn and eventually in need of a major op but I was having some grief with my right knee and my orthopaedic consultant, Mr Kluge said that it was imperative that a full right knee replacement was performed asap. My brother Pete, put up the 8 grand for the op and once again, I was hopping around on sticks!

Coleen had a new job and we split after the shine had gone from our relationship. I was soon seeing Karen, who I referred to as 'Mrs Mad'. She wasn't really mad, just did a few barmy things that got her the title! Karen had plenty of complications in her life at that time and was in the middle of a separation with her husband, 'Swift Nick', who had been in the scooter club with us. That made things somewhat difficult at times but we had some great times nonetheless.

Chapter 15

Once again, I was recovered and back working on shifts with the maintenance at Fields Packaging. I'd been pestering Lindsay for a while trying to get her to come out with me but to no avail. On Mothers Day, I managed to persuade her to have a drink with me and from there, we were soon in a relationship. Now Linds was nearly half my age and a friend of my daughter Lucy (albeit, a few years older) and I'd known her for years really and had seen her grow up from being a teenager into a full grown women. I hadn't really seen her for a few years and now the age gap didn't seem to matter, as we were two adults, with more in common than you could imagine really.

My brother Pete and his wife Sue were solicitors and between them had done well, they'd been on the TV programme, A Place in the Sun and had bought a villa, as a holiday home, on the edge of Barcelona. I had a week out there to get some sun and help them move in, brilliant.

Leeds had had a decent season and it was looking like we were heading straight back up to the Premiership. The play-off final was in Cardiff and we were to play Watford. I headed down to Cardiff on the coach from the 'Branch' with Chaz, Phil, Lindsay's brother Richard and plenty of others. We had a quality day and a good drink, meeting up with Bob Benn and a few others in a pub in Cardiff centre. There was very little sign of the Cardiff City force that had threatened to turn out in numbers to have a set too with Leeds. In fact, there wasn't a great deal of Watford fans about, compared to the vast number of 'Whites'. The game was so one sided, it was unreal. Leeds just didn't turn up and we got battered 3-0. We continued to have a good drink after the game and our coach was one of the last to leave the designated parking area…..another season in the Championship loomed.

My decree absolute eventually came through, so Sue and I said our 'good bye's', we still see each other and get on fine, we had both moved on and both happy in new relationships, all for the best really.

At Fields Packaging, I was on shift with the lads and there was a problem on one of the large Lemanic presses. There was a kind of rumbling noise and the print kept slipping slightly. All the gaffers were there, myself, Matt, Mick Robbo and one or two others. I was holding the encoder unit trying to locate the 'rumble' when the damn thing caught the end of my finger. I pulled away quickly but the end of the finger had been crushed, ripping the nail out completely resulting with blood pouring out of the open wound and the end of the finger hanging on by threads of skin. Once the crowd of people had realised what had happened, blood was splattering onto the floor. Tony Shaw, did a runner at the sight of the claret and big Mark performed the first aid before I headed off to the Infirmary. It was the next day before I was sorted out by the 'Micro-surgeon', the finger was broken in three places and had to be drilled and pinned before the nail could be re-seated and then micro stitching done on each side.!!

Russ and I were spending a lot of time in the Duke William at Shelf but the pub had been taken over by two guys, Richard and Simon. They were partners in every sense! Now I've nothing really against gay people but these two were on a mission to try and change the world for the good of the Gay Rights! It would appear that, in their opinion, quite a lot of 'straight' people were bigoted minded fools and second class citizens compared to them. Even though all the people in the Duke William were making them a healthy living, they would be barring people on a daily basis!

I was having some beers in the Duke with Russ and Jayne one Friday night and apart from ourselves, there were only a hand full of people in the place. Big Jamie was behind the bar but had only been left a couple of C.D's to play and after 3 hours, it was getting pretty tedious on the lugs! He found a Bon Jovi disc and decided to have a change. When the 'couple' arrived back, appearing slightly worse for wear, with their friends, I asked Richard where all the music was for behind the bar and he threw a right wobbler, shouting that myself and Russ thought we owned the village and that both he and Simon were in charge of the pub and could play what music they wanted! Well over the top really………..more than answered the question! He was jumping up and down, throwing a proper tantrum and shouting that it was his house and we had to get out! We were walking up the road when Jamie passed in his car and said that Richard had stated that he was going to give me a good hiding.

Next morning I was bashing on the pub door at 8a.m. There was no way that the guy didn't hear me but he wisely didn't come down to confront me. Apparently he told Ginger Lee later that he hadn't heard me at the door. Even if you're full of 'lush', you should back up what you spout out or do the manly thing and apologise for your actions, either way, stand and be counted.

That lunchtime, Linds and I went to Manchester with a group from Wyke to see Oasis in concert at Eastlands. A good performance and plenty of beers were had. A top band and some great tunes and lyrics and even though I'm not too taken with their choice of footie team, it's better than the red choice!

This was a good year........Linds and I headed up to the Highlands for a break and really got to know each other. Up passed the Lochs to Fort William then Inverness and back down to Edinburgh, stopping off at one or two other idyllic spots on the way. A fantastic week and our relationship was well on track. Shortly after that I had a weekend in Blackpool with a handful of guys from Fields and a couple of the women, Johnny 'Red' Frazer came along with Kinder and although Jamie 'La La' missed the train, he turned up a few hours later....fair play. We had a good old 'do' and "3 sheets to the wind" Austin, picked up a couple of broken ribs for being a cheeky pratt and locking us out of the 'digs'. We had a slight altercation after a group of 'jokers' began to annoy the girls but it panned out ok. I know I'm not on my own when I say that the best bar to frequent for a Saturday afternoon booze up, is the Tower Lounge Bar in Blackpool. Chris almost came a cropper when a group of women became quite angry after he upset their autograph session with one of the Osmond Brothers !!.....good weekend and a day or two to recover!

My top mate Doug and I went to see the Stereophonics in Manchester and had a belting time. We stayed in the city centre at the Midland Hotel .... and we almost missed the start of the concert, as we were in the ale house across the road from the hotel, knocking back a few pints. It was a bit of a seedy hole really, full of dodgy looking fuckers who all seemed to be eyeballing us. We arrived just before the 'Phonics' hit the stage and ended up in decent seats with a quality view. The performance was great and it turned out to be one of the best concerts I'd had the privilege of attending.

Chapter 16

My daughter Lucy had moved out and was on the property ladder, living with her fella, who incidentally, was 'Old Bill'!! I'd been for beers with him on numerous occasions and he wasn't a bad lad, or so it appeared. He'd lived under my roof for a while before they set up home and let's just say, their relationship, could be quite volatile at times. They ended up living together for a year or so before the shit hit the fan and I had to have words before their break-up was finalised.

Linds moved in with me and we had break in the sun out in Tenneriffe. A quality holiday with plenty of sun, good food and reasonably priced drink. The footie was on in a sports bar on the Saturday afternoon and while Linds was still sunning herself by the pool, I went for a few beers and to catch up on the results. Unfortunately, there just happened to be a dozen or so Man U fans in the bar, giving it 'large' and as usual, lowering the tone! I had a few choice words with these 'no-marks' and probably because I was on my own, I didn't get the shite knocked out of me! Lucky. On the Sunday, Linds and I were having a lunchtime tipple and there was the Rangers game on the screen in the bar. I was giving a little support and almost got slapped down by a group of Celtic geezers!!! Best clear off back to Blighty, I thought.!!!

There was an eventful day out when Leeds played away at Ipswich that year. All the lads had tasted a tipple or two before we arrived in Bury St Edmunds, where we had a good couple of hours or more to kill before heading off to Ipswich. Around twelve of us were in the "smallest pub in the world" and it was a tight squeeze! The 'can' was upstairs and the pool table was a miniature on the bar, approximately the size of a block of butter!! A good old time with no trouble, so it was off to the ground. We were close to kick off when we had a problem or two. Dave Barber was refused entry for being bollocksed and when I questioned the lawman, he said that I may as well stand with him as it was obvious we'd both had plenty. Alan Bale thought it was highly funny until he also was halted at the turnstile. We were told to get some food and drink and to smarten up our act. When we returned, ten minutes later, stuffing our faces with burgers, the game had already started and we were confronted by 3 rozzers and half a dozen stewards. One of the lawmen told me to "walk the line" and he would decide whether or not to let us in. I said, "You're having a piss mate, I broke both knees and haven't walked in a straight line for 20 years!!". He apologised profusely and after a brief chat with his 'gang', we were allowed in. It was quite amusing really, we were escorted down the terraces by the ten or so 'yellow coats' to some seats and shortly after, we were almost thrown out for carrying on with some more clever mouthed stewards, Entertaining day to say the least and not a bad result, with us ending up getting a point from the 1-1 draw.

Blaggers was arranging the Stag weekend for Bucko and after coming up with half a dozen different destinations half way around the world, Berlin was to be the venue. Paul was to be the Best Man at Martins wedding so he sorted most of the details out and there was to be a dozen or so of us heading for Deutschland.

Myself, Russ, Bucko, Blaggers, Big Phil, Greeny, Robert, Jason, Raff, Alex, John Poole, Spellers and Andy Minot (a Leeds fan, who for some strange reason, seems to think he's Welsh theses days!), flew from John Lennon airport to Berlin in the search of everything a good Stag Weekend should provide. A full days drinking with myself and Jason ending up in a bar, cut off from the rest and eventually staggering into a taxi at around 5am. I'd met Jason a few years earlier when I was doing a bit of work in Leeds, he was quite a decent 'sparky' and we'd worked alongside each other a few times. We were pretty smashed and walked straight into the glass hotel doors! These were supposedly automatic doors but as we found out later, they were apparently switched to manual on a night. I was rooming with Russ and after a few hours kipping, I was woken by, what I thought was a couple of noisy tractors but it was actually Russ's snoring. Next morning in the square near the Television Tower, live bands were playing and we were knocking back the beers. Blaggers was, to everyone's surprise, clearing tables all over the square, until we found out that there was money back on the glasses…..the cheeky pillock made a mint! Robert was forever on the 'dog' informing his wife of our every move, so I nicknamed him 'Bubbles', a name that has stuck with him, (another quality Elland Road man). He was soon enlightened that weekends away are pretty much a closed book on arrival back in old Britannia. We all know the drill, lap dancing bars, drinking all day and all night and of course, there's always someone who shows a different side to themselves and gets their rocks off.

The Irish bar in the precinct near the hotel was the rendezvous point for our gang and next night, the guys headed a bit further a field by catching a train to the next station. Russ and I were last out and got on the wrong damn train…heading the wrong way! We were in touch on the phones and swapped trains at the next station, only to find out that after we'd left the platform, some lunatic had run riot with a big 'shiv' cutting twenty odd people!!!

The morning we departed was interesting, I'd set the alarm on the phone but hadn't set a time change since we'd landed in Berlin! We were an hour adrift and the taxis were on their way to take us to the airport. Russ was crashing into everything in the room, shouting that his legs were still asleep as we rushed to meet the guys in the foyer. We almost left Greeny at the airport when we boarded the bus after landing but luckily the Bantam fan flagged us down. This was a great few days of drinking with a quality bunch of blokes and we finished off with a good drink back in Shelf.

I was putting in plenty of hours at Fields but was also managing to catch plenty of 'play time' as well. The Red Hot Chilli Peppers were playing at the Don Valley Stadium in Sheffield and myself and Lindsay went along with her cousin Sally and her husband Andy. A tremendous concert from a truly brilliant band, contributing to a great night out. The placed definitely rocked, I would have to say that this band edged out watching Oasis, albeit, not by much though.

Linds and I went to my brother Pete's place near Barcelona for a week or so with them and my brother Bryan and his girlfriend Marie. Pete also took his twins and my mum. Fantastic week was had by all, Barcelona is one of my favourite citys, with eyecatching architecture and a very cosmopolitan culture. Pete and I even found time to use a day to peruse around the Nou Camp Stadium, an exhilarating experience.

My right knee wasn't totally fixed and was giving me a bit of grief and after speaking with the consultant, it was apparent that the new joint had moved and twisted. Great! Now paying for a knee joint isn't like buying a car.....you can't go and ask for the dosh back, so I had to wait two to three months and then have a complete new knee joint replacement yet again. This was to be a more complex operation than the last one, (full joint replacements are bad enough, but far more so when the joint is carrying quite a lot of passed 'baggage').

Field's were sound regarding my time off and I was urged to take my time and get fully fit before returning to work. Even so, I worked hard on the muscles both at home and at a local gym in the endeavour to get sorted as quickly as possible.

For Christmas, we went up to my brother's place. Pete and Sue and the twins had moved to a large house round the corner from Alan Shearer, the footballer, in Ponteland, Newcastle. My mum was also there and we had a great time, really festive and chilled out, good for my recuperation.

My other brother Bryan, living in Dubai, was having his wedding blessed, so we all headed for the airport. Bryan has really done well working for TNT and holds a very good position of status, he can't be faulted and has work hard to get where he is. Lindsay and I were in a villa with my mum, Pete, Sue and the twins, which was a top place with a decent sized pool. My sister Pam, her husband Robert and daughter Hannah were in an apartment and Russ and Jayne were in the Grosvenor Hotel. The main absentee was our nan, who at the age of

97, Dubai was, without a doubt, too great a trek for the old dear to hike.

This was one hell of a get together and the blessing was held in the large winning enclosure at the Jebel Ali Race Course, with the reception to follow at the same venue. This was definitely at the 'top of the tree', an absolutely superb occasion and the heat was roasting.

In the bar area Pete and I were chatting and there was a 'cockney' lad in his mid twenty's who'd obviously had too much 'lush' and was getting louder and louder. A short guy in a sharp suit came in with his missus and started chatting to one of Bryans mates, a big guy called Pele, like the footballer. They were introduced to Pete and I and as soon as the 'loud' lad heard the short guy's accent, he said "What part of the smoke are you from and who do you follow?" the reply was, "East end and I follow West Ham". Well that was a red rag to a bull, as the lad was a Millwall boy and he started mouthing off big style. Pete said to me, "Give the pillock a slap Dave and shut the twat up!" The lad said, "I suppose you're a fucking Leeds fan being a Yorkie". "Too right" I said but before it got out of hand, his uncle pulled him away and removed him from the venue. We didn't need any trouble on that day of all days.

We spent plenty of time with the family and had a brilliant time. Linds and I went over to the Grosvenor Hotel for a meal with Russ and Jayne one evening and was surprised to find Chris Eubank also staying there. We were having a drink I the bar we obliged Chris when he asked to have his picture taken with us, (or was it the other way around?), can't quite remember!

This was to be another very eventful year, in fact each year in this decade was becoming pretty full on. Lindsay was very persistent regarding the fact that she wanted a child and after many discussions and in depth conversations, Linds became pregnant.

Fields had lost the big orders from their main clients and were cutting the workforce. The maintenance department would need to be cut by two bodies. Big Shaun was emigrating 'down under' and taking into consideration the time I'd taken off because of the operations, I thought it was best for me to accept redundancy rather than be pushed, so I volunteered and left in the middle of the year.

Shaun and I had a night out in Huddersfield with the lads from Fields but the festivities didn't end too well for myself. We'd all drunk plenty and had been split up into different groups. I was in a gaff with Blandy, Travs, Dude and Big Rob, none of whom were fighting lads. Now Rob is a big guy, around 6ft 3ins and I suppose he could be pretty dangerous if pushed to the edge but it's not in his make up, the other three chaps just aren't in the 'biscuit tin'. There was a tall black kid, on a par with Rob for size, probably in his early twenties and he was strutting about saying that everyone was eyeballing his 'skirt' and basically trying to push someone into having a dig with him. We told him no-one was interested and that nobody was interested in his girl. He was really persistent and said he was going to slap Dude, so I told him to back off and as he raised his mits, I half got a punch in but didn't connect fully. I have no idea if this kid was on drugs or was a boxer, or both but I have never been hit as hard and as quick in my life. It didn't matter which way I ducked, weaved or moved, he was connecting constantly with combination shots. I went down on one knee and grabbed the front of his shirt, thinking that if I pulled him in close, I get to grips with the bastard. Well, think again; the fuckers shirt was off and the combination shots landed as hard and as fast as ever! The doormen eventually grabbed the guy and launched him out, his handful of mates following him out of the door. One of the doormen said that he'd acting up for a couple of hours and thought he was on some gear, to which I thought, maybe they could have done their job and 'binned' him earlier, saving me from getting knocked about! I think I landed around four shots on him and probably took around twenty from him! I wasn't too agile on the old pins and even though I've overcome in excess of a couple of thousand confrontations in my life, it was time to 'clock out'! I was ok really, a bit battered and bruised and the damn nose bone broken for the tenth time but nothing too serious and we still managed a few more 'jars' before heading home.

Chapter 17

Linds and I got married in Gretna Green on the 26th July 2007 and I couldn't believe my luck. Here was a beautiful young woman, nearly half my age marrying me and due to give birth to our son in a few months time...... fantastic, I couldn't have been happier. Russ and Jayne had come up to Gretna to witness the wedding and just to be there for us really, nothing too elaborate but everything we wanted. After the wedding day, the two of us spent the week in Scotland, with no distractions, just driving around and staying in some lovely hotels.

I went back to the bakery in Leeds as a Deputy Engineering Manager but the position didn't last long. Apparently there was a court hearing coming up and the purse strings had to be tightened, so my job was one of the first to be axed. I wasn't too happy at the time but the birth of our son George, soon put the job situation well in the shade. There was a slight matter for concern which led to the birth becoming a matter of urgency when the baby became stressed. The midwives had incompetently ruled out Lindsay's claim that her waters had broken hours earlier, even although three of them had examined her! A female doctor was on the scene and luckily, she was more up on her game than the midwives and George was born fit and healthy. The initial bond between baby and parent is something that cannot really be described or compared to but one proverb is one hundred percent correct:-

"Children are a poor man's treasure!"

My nan had been diagnosed with cancer and at 97 years old, we all knew it was just a matter of time. The whole family had no doubts that she would pass the one hundred mark, so it was a massive shock when the cancer kicked in. Nan just carried on as though she was fit and well, not wanting anyone to make a fuss or treat her any different, she was one tough and independent old bird! The look on her face was indescribable when we took George to see her, to bring so much happiness to someone with no real effort, is a total joy that not be compared to.

Over Christmas, my brother Pete said they were going into the 'holiday let' business and he wanted me to work for them, renovating properties and bringing them up to a 'letting' standard.

I would drive up to Northumberland on a Monday, work until Friday afternoon and then drive back down to Linds and George. It was hard work but satisfying and enjoyable, although the strain was showing on Lindsay due to time we were spending apart. We decided to put the gears in motion, with the view to relocating up in the sticks in Northumberland.

Nan passed away just prior to her 98th birthday and it was definitely a big blow to us all. The woman was a sheer inspiration to every one who knew her. We had visions of her outliving us all, such was her bond with life and her determination to overcome every obstacle that crossed her path. My brother Pete's wife Sue, wrote a nice letter to the Queen explaining that nan would have easily passed the hundred mark if the cancer hadn't suddenly kicked in and was so looking forward to receiving the much sort after telegram. She received a nice reply in the form of a letter from one of the Queen's aides expressing Her Majesty's condolences.

Leeds had had a reasonable season and met Carlisle in the play-offs. I was working in Alnmouth, Northumberland, a great little place quite near to Alnwick, where some of the Harry Potter filming was done. I was staying at the property that I was working on and was watching the play off match in a local pub called the Sun. Leeds hit the winner with a few minutes to go and I hit the roof! The whole pub stopped and stared at the lunatic, jumping up and down and shouting at the top of his voice. The landlord just said that the quiz was starting shortly and not to mind the Neanderthal Leeds bloke!!

There's an old saying………………..
"Tha can allus tell a Yorkshireman but tha can't tell him much bart owt !"……………….especially when he's celebrating victory involving his footie team!

The New Wembley was the venue as Leeds played Doncaster for a place in the next tier and the hallowed ground was swamped with a white blanket as the Leeds masses filled London. There was reported to be over one hundred thousand Leeds fans in the capital on the day of the play-off final and expectations were high. There were large gaps in the Doncaster sectors and half a dozen of us managed to get in their 'end' behind the goal. It wasn't long before a couple of hundred 'Whites' were grouped in the area but the law were soon in there with an equal number. We were totally surrounded by the 'plod' and weren't even allowed to access any of the facilities. Come half time, we were ushered out in two's to use the toilets and under the stands, were lines of Riot Cops!! We blew the game and lost 1-0, what a nightmare.........stuck in the shitty division for another season, profoundly heartbreaking!

Linds, George and myself went to live in a beautiful little village called Embleton, a few miles from Alnwick. The bungalow was quite large and had spacious lawned gardens at both the back and front. The location was ideal for me to work from, taking into consideration that there was a company property at Alnmouth and one at Seahouses, both approximately 8 miles from Embleton. We loved the location, there are 2 pubs, a pub/restaurant, hotel, church, Post Office and local store, with a five minute walk down to the beach. The accent there was sometimes a little difficult to get to grips with, as a few folk spoke with the 'Border' twang, which is a mix of accents. Nevertheless, the locals were nice people and easy to get on with.

My mate Paul 'tatey' Hayton was fifty and to celebrate the occasion, we were to have a 30 strong excursion to Prague! We were on two large mini busses and the atmosphere was 'tops', until we hit a snag on the motorway. There had been some kind of smash and the delays were horrendous. The first bus managed to get to the East Midlands airport on time but the second was caught up in major traffic and half a dozen mobile phones were red hot, trying to get something sorted at the check in desks. The airport staff were great and extended the check-in time by around 45 minutes for us, so, panic over and we all managed to board.

We hit the 'lush' as soon as we arrived in Prague, while a couple of the lads sorted out the digs. The apartment block was, let's say, ... different! I was in an apartment that had half a dozen rooms, with Russ,

Greigy, his son Pat and Sean Gorman. There was plenty of room really but the place was nothing to write home about, albeit, adequate for lads on the booze. The floor below us was flooded out the next day, after a waste pipe backed up and there was human waste everywhere. It's funny to think of it now but at the time, it was a nightmare for Roger, Stocky, Carl and the rest of the guys on that level.

For those of you that have never been to Prague, half of the city is sound and buzzing and the other half is a shit hole! The alcohol prices reflect the part of the city that you're in really, although there are plenty of dodgy fuckers in all areas. England's footie team was playing Kazakhstan and we were in a big boozer in the decent side of the city, drinking like it was going out of fashion! After England had won the game 5-1, Mick and Stocky were 'leathered' and got a taxi to take them back to the digs. Half an hour later, they were wondering around outside the same pub!! Apparently the taxi bloke had charged them around thirty quid, drove the dim fuckers in a large circle and dropped them back at the pick up spot!! You could not make it up in your dreams!! There were plenty of Black guys outside the bars trying to entice us in with various drinks offers etc but the most outrageous chat line was, "Do you want to see a monkey shagging a dwarf?". Mal and Phil were in hysterics after being thrown this line and Mal was almost physically sick at the thought! Needless to say, nobody paid to view the event!

A couple of local hookers ended up in the apartment block and two of our guys were left with considerable amounts of cash missing from their wallets due to 'ladies' light fingers! There were plenty more incidents on that quality trip, with Reynolds and John Marlow venturing into a local bar in a less desirable area. After being eyeballed for a few minutes, two of the dozen or so dodgy looking fuckers got up and locked the main doors. The landlord went barmy, shouting and carry on at the blokes, before opening the doors and quickly shoving John and Ian out onto the street. The silly bastards went back the next day to 'show face' and the landlord give them a round of 'fucks', telling them to clear off while they still could! The morning we were due to leave, I was outside the apartments and a fucking great fish came from nowhere and hit me on the shoulder!! I lost it slightly, screaming at the top of my voice but nobody stuck there head out of a window to own up to the 'flying fish'. I had to get washed, changed and dump the stinking shirt only to find out later that it was Hayton who had randomly launched the fish straight out of the window into the street and not at me (supposedly!).

We returned to The Harp of Erin pub in Bradford, where most of the guys had a few beers before heading off home. There were plenty of folk in there for a Monday evening and most of them were lashed up. Two 'old boys' were threatening to have a piece of each other, one of whom was dressed in a smart suit, shirt and tie. The 'suited' geezer fell over backwards, landed on his arse beneath table that had a few drinks on it. The table rocked and a full pint tipped over, covering the old fellows head, soaking the silly pillock through!! Both myself and Hayton were actually crying with laughter, it was one of the funniest things I had ever witnessed in my life!

The right knee was giving me a bit of grief and after seeing the consultant in Northumberland, it was bad news. Apparently there was an infection in the knee and the full joint had to be removed, which was massive set back for me. The joint was taken out and a 'spacer' put in place to keep the Femur, the Tibia and the Fibula apart. The leg was then pumped full of antibiotics and I was hopping around on crutches for three full months! When the consultants were sure that the infection was well and truly gone, The 'spacer', all scar tissue and what was left of any ligaments were removed and a full chrome joint implemented. So there I was, with yet another 30 plus staples in my limb but on the mend again, or so I thought! I was managing to get around without crutches but had some really bad pains in the left leg and went to get checked out. The staff at A&E at Wansbeck hospital said that I damaged the tissues in my and sent me packing, advising me to rest. A couple of days later, I couldn't stand on the leg and returned to the hospital. They rushed me in an ambulance to Newcastle's Freeman hospital stating that there was no blood flow into the foot and I was in serious danger of losing the leg. I had to have a vein/artery graft because the femaral posterior tibial artery had blocked and I was in surgery for around nine hours. The worst case scenario was amputation of the lower leg or the loss of two or three toes. The operation was deemed a success and the sense of relief when waking to find both lower limbs still intact is indescribable. So it was a case of resting the leg in the hospital for a week and that meant around a hundred mile trip for Linds and the boy each day..... not ideal.

Chaz dropped everything and came straight up from "God's own County" to visit me and see if there was anything I needed. He spent a good couple of hours at the bedside and then set off back home, a top man! Another top geezer that turned up out of the blue was Doug. He'd apparently come over from Spain to see family and visit his old man's grave in Northumberland, whereupon, he thought he'd call in on Linds and myself. It was a nice surprise when the big fella walked into the hospital ward clutching a bunch of grapes!

I was recovering well but developing properties was becoming harder as the market was tight and the prices had stabilised, I realistically knew that we would have to contemplate moving back down to Yorkshire. People always state that working for family is, most of the time, a no-go area and I can only say that I gave it my best shot but it was just not meant to be. Not to worry, there was no 'fall out' or anything like that, we just called it a day and it was back down 'home'. Pete thought the country was going down the tubes and was looking to move abroad with Sue and the boys.

My daughter Lucy married Robin and I couldn't have hoped for a better son-in –law. The wedding was a plush event and quite a few people put the effort in to ensure that, mainly Lucy's mum Sue. Walking down that aisle and giving my daughter away was a really proud and prestigious moment for me. My baby was all grown up and I think that her mother and I had done a half decent job in assisting that. I reckon that my 'Father's speech' went down quite well, I received a good round of applause and no boos and hope I did them proud. I remember thinking that even though I'd been a Best Man four times, giving a speech as the Father of the bride was the most difficult.

We had settled up in Northumberland and it was a sad time to have to move back down to Yorkshire but we must all look forward and not dwell on what might have been, I am a firm believer that everything has a purpose and everything happens for a reason.

A person has to stand by what they say, a man's word is his bond and he can be measured by the strength of his word. Now, this isn't always the case with certain people, I have noticed this more so since I have returned to the area. There are one or two guys around here who seriously need to take a good look at themselves.

There are half a dozen people that said they wouldn't have a problem in sorting me a job out but when the push came to the shove, 'the shouts turned to whispers'. Some people are so full of themselves really and speak before thinking it through, so you should never rely on the promises unless you're sure that they can become reality because as I've experienced, you can end up missing the safety net! My so-called mate Eddie is the most disappointing of the bunch, after all we went through working together, he totally let me down after verbally promising me a management position and then didn't even bother to answer any of my phone calls or reply to my emails…… "You broke my heart Fredo!" Karma mate Karma. What goes round, comes around and I don't think I have to put any more names in the frame, the other guys know who they are. Never promise what you can't deliver because you can end up looking a complete twat or just an everyday 'gobshite'. Greigy stood tall and was as strong as his word, he managed to push a bit of work my way, even though his business has been through the mill and he's struggled……top man. So there I was, working as self employed, just doing a little bit and still spending plenty of time with my wife and lad.

That year the season had gone well for the Whites and ended with us clinching promotion to the Championship with a 2-1 home win over Bristol Rovers. The game was so-so but the result was priceless. I was sat with Phil Mc, Mally and Chris Mann and after the game, we had a bloody good drink with Hayton and a few of the other guys............. a massive season for us and a step closer to getting back into the Premiership.

I've spent more time with George than I ever did with my daughter Lucy, when she was his age, more to the working calendar than anything else. Time never stands still for any man and we must live each day as it comes and make the most of what we have.

I was getting pain from a lump in the top of my right thigh, which was a result of the surgery I'd had on the leg. The doctors had said that it was glandular and nothing to worry about but it was aching and I needed it checking out. The scan result came through and the report stated that it was probably cancerous. This was a blow like I'd never felt before, I was numbed, my thoughts were a blur and I honestly thought that this was a bridge too far.... I was shitting it. England played the USA in the World Cup, drawing 1-1 (pathetic) and after the game I sat down with Russ and confided in him regarding the predicament I was in. Hence to say, we had a damn good drink, shed a tear or two and I told him this could be a TKO for me. The next day, Linds, George and I went up to the North East coast for a 'chill out' week and when we returned, I was in for a biopsy. The whole of the lump was accessible, so the surgeon cut the lot out, stating that he didn't think it was a cancerous but obviously couldn't confirm that until the thing had been to the lab. I sat in the hospital and watched England's poor performance against Slovenia while pondering my position. A few days later and the results were back, Linds and myself were down at the McMillan hospital and the doctor confirmed that the growth wasn't cancerous and I didn't have to have any further treatment. The relief of being given that kind of news is priceless; a statement that money could not buy, the weight that was lifted from my shoulders can not be measured. We may sometimes wallow in self pity and we all have a moan from time to time but we should all count our blessings and give thanks for the good things in our lives. I may occasionally come across as quite aggressive and bad tempered at times but since that day, I really do portray life in a different light and except there are always plenty of people a lot worse off than us. My mother has beaten cancer twice and I cannot imagine the trauma that she endured.

The vascular team at the hospital stated that they were happy with the artery graft and signed me off, stating that no further scans or tests were needed, which was a relief.

I had a new knee cap fit to the right knee through choice, which went well and feels quite good, as the last one was moving about a little and giving me some pain. I can speak of some of the operations I've had as though they were something you bought over the counter at the local supermarket but I have no doubt that to the normal bloke on the street, they would be a daunting obstacle to face. I'm definitely not trying to come across as a clever or condescending prick, these are just fences on the racecourse of my life.

So here we are, 2011, treading the boards of existence......... health's good, I have a super wife, a fantastic young son and a lovely daughter, who is now a grown woman building her own life. I'd like to think that I'm a good husband, as well as a great dad and hope that I'm perceived to have been a decent colleague to all those that I've worked alongside and by my present work colleagues.

Life is as hard as we make it, we shouldn't dwell on the past, only look to the future whilst enjoying and making the most of what we now have in the present. As the saying goes; "We fall down in order to learn how to get back up!"

Below are listed, a few of the guys that served with me when I was a member of the greatest Scooter Club ever formed.

The Doormen listed are but a few of the lads that I either worked alongside or were in my employ and I'd like to take the opportunity to thank them for all their efforts and time, operating in an environment that very rarely gives out accolades. I must apologise to all the lads that 'stood' with me that I've overlooked and aren't named. Long time friends in general don't need to be 'listed', "you'll always be there fellas" and remember …….. "The strongest weapon of all, is the heart of a volunteer!"

Bradford Scooter Club

Stuart Drake	Russ Hodgson	Andy Womersley
Duggie Johnson	Steve 'Jock' Johnson (RIP)	Jeff Johnson
Brian Hudson	Dave Watson (Winker)	Zippy
Dave (Boy) Evans	Dean Halmshaw	Andy Russian
Ian Fearnley	Don Fearnley	Ian Parkin
Paul Greig	Malcolm Nelson	Chris Doherty
Ducka	Simmo	Glen Parkin
Stuart Royston (Berwyn)	Nick Finnigan (Swift Nick)	Tony Finnigan
Dave Allen	Chris Wormold	Kevin Hodgson
Steve Mullaney (Joe 90)	Bob (Hairy) Gledhill	Andy Ryan
Anthony (Buzz) Beaumont	Tony Mann	Ray the baker
'Quiet' Steve	Dave Myers (RIP)	Sean McNulty
Paul Peterson	Dave Suter	Dave Smith
'Sneaker'	'Ron Miller'	'Shipley' Glen

Doormen

Gary Kinder	Dean Loynes	Trevor Cruxon
Paul Airey	Jimmy Donnally	Martin Poutney
Geoff Watson	Paul Hamson	Billy Hamson
Mark Zamma	Graham Nalton	Bob Siree
Ian Siree	John Pye	Alan Mullaney
Roger	Garffy	Richard
'Tattooed' Barry	Dave Holmes	Farrouke
Jim Goodall	Gary Wilson	Andy Long
'Black' Tony	Tony Lumb	Jason
Abby	Simon	Pete Tidswell
'Poney-tail' Mark	Piotre	Steve Spalding
John Spalding	Morgan Duffy	Nathan
Jay	Big John	Slick
Hardy	Nicky Muff	Joe 90
Kev Hodgson	Mick	Danny Donlon
Paul Rigby	Jamie	Robin
Big Tony	Tebor	Max
Tom	Ozzy	Stevie
Ivan	Steve Chapman	Richard Butcher
Huddy	Dave York	Scotty
Chris	Sean	Budgie
Chalmers	Dave Flynn	Lionel
Darrell	Keith	Bri Pollard